All is Well With My Soul Daily Devotions

Vera Simpson Gaines

AuthorHouse™
1663 Liberty Drive, Suite 200
Bloomington, IN 47403
www.authorhouse.com
Phone: 1-800-839-8640

© 2008 Vera Simpson Gaines. All rights reserved.

No part of this book may be reproduced, stored in a retrieval system, or transmitted by any means without the written permission of the author.

First published by AuthorHouse 11/25/2008

ISBN: 978-1-4389-3021-3 (sc)

Library of Congress Control Number: 2008910150

Printed in the United States of America
Bloomington, Indiana

This book is printed on acid-free paper.

Cover imagery by Doug McClure

Dedication Page

This book is dedicated to my loving mother who raised me in a Christian home. The following poem was written in honor of her.

MOTHER

She stood only 5'7",

but was a tower of strength.

She had the leadership of Peter,

the patience of Job,

the persistence of Paul,

the compassion of Jesus,

the innocence of Mary,

the wisdom of scholars,

the talents of God,

and the love of all.

I called her, Mother.

Vera S. Gaines

Introduction

In December 2007, I was told I had macular degeneration disease. Weeks later I had an appointment in Memphis, TN with a retina specialist. Not only did he find two yellow spots in the center of my vision but found 10-12 spots in the outer area. He diagnosed me with hereditary drusen and said I was actually too young to have MD. I will be checked every year and if any more spots show up then that will be macular degeneration disease.

While I was waiting for my appointment, I realized that people facing adversities need a daily devotion book to help them through their storms. I searched through the bible and found encouraging scriptures that give hope and promise for a better tomorrow. No matter what you're facing, the following devotions will confirm to you that you are not alone in your suffering. Claim God's promises and move forward in life. Keep busy doing the Lord's work because time is very short. God bless you in all that you do. Remember you can not have rainbows without the storm.

Vera S. Gaines

January 1

Good Works

Being confident of this very thing, that he which hath begun a good work in you will perform it until the day of Jesus Christ.
Philippians 1:6

    I've noticed that some people will do good works and then retire themselves from work at church or in the community. As Christians we are responsible for the spreading of the good news and helping the needy, especially widows in our families or church or community. There is no cut off date that tells us that we can now relax and that our work is done. When you work for the Lord, the work is never done.

    Time is very short for us here on earth when compared to eternity. Some people believe that good works will earn them a place in heaven. You are saved by grace. You don't earn your salvation. If you are truly a serious Christian, you will want to do good works until the day the Lord calls you home.

    What can you do today for our Lord?

January 2

Child Of God

Yet the Lord longs to be gracious to you; He rises to show you compassion. For the Lord is God of justice. Blessed are all who wait for Him!

Isaiah 30:18

    This verse is very important for people to understand because there are so many hurting people who think no one loves them. No one loves like the Lord. He longs to spend the day with you and greets you with a sunrise and welcomes you into each day with the singing of birds and the fragrance of flowers. He kisses you goodnight with the glow of the moonlight and a gentle breeze in your hair. He watches over you while you sleep. He orders angels to protect you from harm. The Lord wants you to talk to Him through prayer and quiet times. He wants you to study His word. He sits with you all the time. You are never alone.

    Take a few minutes and notice the presence of God.

January 3

The Heart

Man judges by the outward appearance but God judges the heart.
unknown

Some people would say the brain is the most important organ in the human body. I say the heart is more important. If one doesn't have a good heart, it doesn't matter how smart the brain is. If one has a good heart then the brain will be put to good use.

A good heart will see the need in the church, community, and world. A good heart will stop and help a stranger in need along the side of the road. A good heart will think to say kind things to others. A good heart will give others what they need without them having to ask. God loves a good heart because it will reveal the love of Him to those who don't know Him. People will know we are Christians by our love.

Show God's love to everyone you meet today.

January 4

Fear

If you fear God, you should not fear anything else.

Beth Moore

I think it is healthy to have a fear of God. God made everything you see and He decides when and why and what happens. He is in total control and there is nothing or no one who can change that. As long as you are living the life God created you to be then there should be no fear of what's to come.

God knows what's best for us even when we don't. So when God closes a window or shuts a door, don't fear the unknown. Put everything in God's hands and let Him work out the details. You just show up for duty.

Fear is a four-letter word. Don't let it keep you from your purpose in life.

Today I want you to face your fear head on with the help of God.

January 5

Faith

We walk by faith, not by sight.

2 Corinthians 5:7(NASB)

Those of us who have lost vision can understand this verse the best. Faith is believing what can not be seen.

There are people who were fortunate enough to live in Jesus' time here on earth. They saw Him. They walked with Him. They ate with Him. We have not laid eyes on Him but we know He lives. We know God exist but we have not seen Him. We know heaven exist but we have not been there, yet. Why do we believe?

I was blessed because I had a mother who insisted that we attend church every Sunday. It was in church that I learned to love Jesus Christ and God. I learned how much they love me, also.

In my latter years, I have learned the most. In 2000, I was told I had a very rare tumor behind my left eye and I would lose my vision in the eye forever. Two years later I had to have the eye removed. My vision in my right eye is steadily growing worse. Time and time again, I'm learning to walk by faith and not by sight. I could have folded my arms and dropped into depression but I have pressed on because I know God can use me. No matter what your skills or talents, God can use you in a mighty way.

Find something you can do today for God.

January 6

Heavenly Thoughts

Let heaven fill your thoughts. Do not think only about things down here on earth

Colossians 3:2 (NLT).

When I was a child in Sunday school, I loved hearing about heaven. I was the child who asked a million questions. Even though there's a lot about heaven in the Bible, it still wasn't enough for me. I spent a lot of time day dreaming about heaven.

When my mother died, I spent countless hours picturing her in the presence of Jesus. It was the only thing that helped keep me sane at the time.

Can you imagine what it's going to be like to look into the eyes of Jesus for the very first time? I imagine it will take my breath away. To hear His voice for the very first time saying, "Welcome, home my faithful servant."

Heaven, a place where there is no pain, sorrows, crying, or troubles. The last shall be first. What an awesome experience it will be!

Think on these things.

January 7

Forever

Jesus Christ the same yesterday, and today, and forever.
Hebrews 13:8

    In a fast changing world, it's comforting to know that some things never change. Every few minutes we have millions of cells that are changing in our bodies. Everything we own is decaying. Relationships change. Times change. Jobs change but the most important thing is Jesus Christ will never change. He'll always be our Father. He'll never forsake us or abandon us like so many others. You can count on Him every single time.

    Jesus is not in heaven twitting His fingers. He's praying for you. Jesus is the only one you can count on. He is your compass. Let Jesus change your life for the better.

January 8

Comfort

You are with me; your rod and staff, they comfort me.
Psalm 23:4 (NKJV)

    I learned this verse as a child and it has carried me all the days of my life. Your rod and your staff speaks of leadership and strength. You picture a shepherd leading his flock. When one goes astray the shepherd won't rest until that one lamb is back in the fold. He cares so much for you. He cares more for you than anyone else cares for you. Ask yourself what you can do for Him. After all He gave His life up for you so that you could have eternal life with Him in heaven.

    What will you do for Christ today?

January 9

Ministry

But watch thou in all things, endure afflictions, do the work of an evangelist, make full proof of thy ministry.
2 Timothy 4:5

As we get older, we start thinking about the time that we have left to accomplish the things that we have wanted to do before our time is up. Since we have no notice of when that departure will be, we should be knocking things off our list now.

My husband and I have always said when we retire, we're going to work on mission projects. Unfortunately, we have waited so late that I'm now disabled and unable to travel. I work behind the scenes and now he goes in my place. He just returned from a 10-day trip to Ghana to help with a leadership conference and help build a church in memory of my parents. So even if you are unable to travel like me, you can still be a part of missions by donating. God is counting on you.

Ask God today what He would like for you to do for Him.

January 10

Perilous Times

This know also, that in the last days perilous times shall come.
2 Timothy 3:1

Talk about perilous times. The weather has been wild for 2008 with more tornadoes in the spring than all of 2007. Now the mid west is flooding and it breaks my heart to see the houses floating down the river. People are losing everything they own. Earthquakes are rocking China and Japan while Myanmar has been devastated by a typhoon. By the way things are going, I dread to see this year's hurricane season. As if that weren't enough, we've got wildfires burning in the west.

What does the Bible say about perilous times? It says things will get worse as time grows short. Who should we lean on? The one and only rock of all ages. We are to run under His wings as little chicks run to their mother for protection. Christ loves us and cares deeply for us.

Therefore, we should not fear anything. Remember Job.

Even though he lost everything, including his children, God restored him in time. Job was faithful to God even in adversity.

What can you do today to prepare yourself for perilous times?

January 11

Promise

But continue thou in the things which thou hast learned and hast been assured of knowing of whom thou hast learned them.
2 Timothy 3:14

There's one reassuring thing we've learned from all our Bible study and teachings are that God does not lie. We can take His promises to the bank. You can't say that about anyone else you know. Humans will fail you, but God will stay true to His word.

It's tough at the time of trials and tribulations, but we come out the other side wiser and stronger for the experience.

Tough times will come. The question is will you use the word of God to survive it?

January 12

Faith

Faith is the substance of things hoped for, the evidence of things not seen.

Hebrews 11:1 (NKJV)

What kind of faith do you have? In today's times, it requires a lot of faith just to survive. Christianity is constantly being challenged and attacked by unbelievers and false prophets. Christians are being persecuted every day. It's my faith that allows me to deal with a wicked world. God will one day say to His Son, "Go get them!" We will be taken to paradise to live with our Lord and Savior forever. Nothing can keep you or me from our promised paradise. So whatever you are going through right now, it won't last.

While I'm waiting to meet Jesus face to face, I'm busy building His kingdom. Time is running short. The clock is ticking toward a final end of things, as we know it.

I'm watching the "Great Commission" come true as Christianity spreads south of the equator. Once the world has heard the good news then our Lord will return.

Are you ready?

January 13

Near

What great nation has a God as near to them as the Lord our God is near to us?

Moses

If you were asked to make a list of five people who are most important to you, where on that list would God be? Most would probably have God listed last. Where should God be in the scheme of things? The answer should be number one on the list. Nothing and no one should ever come before God.

What does your checkbook tell you? Your checkbook will tell you where you spend most of your time. If you will make God number one in your life, you will see the world in a whole different light.

God wants to be ever so near to you. He misses you when you rush off to work with not even a word. He longs to talk to you during the day. How do you think He feels when you collapse in bed without saying your prayers or thanking Him for the beautiful day He created just for you? I'm sure He feels crushed.

Today, I want you to think of ways that will draw you closer to God on a daily basis. What a difference it'll make.

I love knowing I have the most powerful God on my side.

Who has your back?

January 14

Close By

Paul, He is not far from each of us.

Acts 17:27(NIV)

We all know Paul had a thorn in his side but nowhere in the Bible does it say what that thorn was in his flesh. I think we were not told so more people could relate to Paul. I consider my three different kinds of arthritis a thorn in the bones. I suffer with pain every day, but I remind myself that Paul continued on his road to furthering the kingdom, no matter how he felt. Time does not stand still for anyone. Even though I'm disabled that doesn't give me a pass on what needs to be done. It's not an excuse to sit at home and do nothing.

There are times that I've actually felt God's presence. If you sincerely want to feel His presence, ask Him to make Himself known and see what happens. You may be very surprised.

January 15

Sure Bet

I will not leave you.

Genesis 28:15

This verse is so important to so many people because abandonment is the source of pain for so many people, especially children who were abandoned by their parents. This act alone has caused untold damage to countless people all over the world. This is the kind of damage that effects one's self esteem and relationship issues well into adult years. Marriages have broken up because one partner can not trust the other partner to stay for the length of the marriage.

We all know how important trust is in any relationship. People may come and go but one constant you can totally trust is that God will not abandon you. If anyone has moved in the relationship, it's you.

In order to keep yourself close to God, it's extremely important that you obey God and keep Him at the top of your list of priorities. Once that has been achieved, you will find that life flows a whole lot easier. You will see that a lot of things fall by the wayside that once upon a time you thought were important to your daily life. Learn to guard yourself by the music that you listen to and the TV programs that you watch. Also watch who you hang around. Our friends were the first things that changed.

What will you change today?

January 16

Restful Soul

Take my yoke upon you and learn from me, for I am gentle and lowly in heart, and you will find rest for your souls.
Matthew 11:29 (NKJV)

    Jesus is telling us to take His word as instruction on how to live and act. Jesus was very mild mannered, but could be forceful when it was needed. Remember the scene at the temple when He threw out the moneychangers? The people were buying and selling items like a market place. The church was no place for this activity. Jesus became very angry and it was justified in this instance.

    There is a great deal of angry people walking around today. The reasons are as varied as the people are. Road rage is a perfect example of people with short fuses. The term "postal" is used when an employee goes off the deep end and takes the lives of people they worked with. We hear story after story about people who lost their temper. Jesus tells us we need to control our temper. Most people think their temper is justified. Jesus says we'll find peace if we can control our emotions. If you'll ask God to help you in this department, He'll be more than happy to help you because you are willing to become more like Him.

    What can you do today to become more like Christ?

January 17

God's Sufficiency

Jesus said, "With men it is impossible, but not with God, because all things are possible with God."

Mark 10:27

How many times have we made the decision to handle things on our own? I know I grew up with the mentality that I' ll just fix it myself and not bother anyone else. I can't tell you how many times I made things worse. The numbers are high. We think God is too busy to handle our problems, but that's not the case. God wants us to come to Him with all our problems. If your request matches up with God's will, then you're in business. God knows what's best for us even when we don't, so don't expect God to answer all your prayers. Sometimes His answer is no. It doesn't hurt to ask. I had to ask God to help me to forgive some people in my life that I had not been able to forgive on my own. I was amazed at how quickly He helped me. This was something God had wanted me to turn over to Him for years, so I'm sure He was so happy to finally hear me beg Him for help. I could hear Him say, "Finally!"

January 18

Godliness

Godliness is beneficial in every way, since it holds promise for the present life and also for the life to come.
1 Timothy 4:8

What is godliness? Webster's dictionary says it's the quality or state of being godly.

Do you know of some godly people in your life? It's very important to surround yourself with godly people but remember they are human, also. They will make mistakes. There was only one perfect person who walked on this earth and that was Jesus.

As wicked as this world is, there are some very godly people still here. Most people think it's an unattainable goal to be Christ like but it is possible and it's something we need to reach for. Can it be done over night? No! With the right attitude, there are things that you can work on every day to make this goal possible. Setting goals is a step in the right direction. Start with short-range goals and decide what negative habits need to go first. Examples are controlling your language, eliminate music that sings about drinking and other bad things, and refuse to watch R-rated movies or TV programs. That's a very good start. You'll see a big difference with just these three goals. Don't stop there. Continue to look honestly at your life and make the necessary changes to become more Christ like. You'll love the new you!

January 19

Beginnings

Throw off all the transgressions you have committed, and make yourselves a new heart and a new spirit.

Ezekiel 18:31

First, let's define transgressions. Transgressions are an act or process, or instance of transgressing, infringement or violation of a law, command, or duty. Some one who chooses to constantly break the law or not respect authority because they think they are above the law is a narcissist. In other words, a person who is in love with self. They think the world revolves around them and that they should be the center of everything that is going on. With this kind of attitude, one can not help others because they are too focused on self. To serve the Lord, you have to die to self. Once this happens you will develop a new heart and a new spirit. You will develop a new sense and be able to recognize where there is a need; when before you might not have noticed at all. You will love the new you and so will God. So get busy and become the person God created you to be. Nothing like the beginning of a new year to set some new and improved resolutions.

January 20

Fatherly Love

Lord you have heard the desire of the humble; you will strengthen their hearts. You will listen carefully.

Psalm 10:17

Jesus is always listening. That is so important to me because I've had people in my life that would walk out of the room while I was in the middle of telling them something. That is so disrespectful. Jesus loves you enough that He would not do that to you. Jesus knows we depend on Him and need Him at all hours of the day or night. He loves it when we spend time with Him. You won't get a busy signal when you call on Him. You won't get voicemail, either.

One good trait of a good Christian is being a very good listener. It's so easy in today's world to be caught up in the business of life. That's what Satan wants you to be, is too busy to talk to God or to study His word. Confusion is his middle name. Tell Satan to hit the road going south!

Soak up some fatherly love today.

January 21

Cancer

What cancer cannot do...
It can not invade the soul,
suppress memories
kill friendship,
destroy peace
conquer the spirit,
shatter hope,
cripple love,
corrode faith,
steal eternal life,
silence courage.
unknown

I saw this saying in a catalog and it moved me. My mother battled cancer for five years before losing her life at age 50. She had such a great attitude in the midst of adversity. What allowed her to be so positive? Her Christian faith carried her through. She had her eyes on Jesus and she kept the focus. She knew what was waiting for her on the other side. She also knew her sister who died at age 9 from pneumonia and her father who died several years before would greet her at the gate.

If you've read all the descriptions in the Bible about heaven, you would give praise everyday for being one day closer to paradise. Everything here will be destroyed.

January 22

The End

'When I stand before God at the end of my life, I would hope that I would have not a single bit of talent left and could say, "I used everything you gave me." '

Erma Bombeck

I love this saying from Erma Bombeck because that's how I feel. When I go home, I want to know that I did everything God expected of me. I want to hear, "Welcome, home my faithful servant."

It's not too late for you to start doing charity work. Pray for God to reveal to you, what He would have you to do for Him. There are so many out there that could use help. All you have to do is look.

Today is a good day to start!

January 23

Heart Healing

"The Lord is my strength and my shield; my heart trusts in Him, and I am helped, Therefore my heart rejoices, and I praise Him with my song."
Psalm 28:7

Every time I've had serious health problems, I amerce myself in the book of Psalms. No matter what the news is, I rejoice with my Lord in song. Even though I've lost an eye and I'm losing vision in my one and only, I can still sing!

My Lord has carried me through some serious problems and I always come out the other side stronger because I know God will take care of me and will until my last breath. If you listen to other people's problems, you will still want to go home with your problems instead of theirs. This is where count your blessings comes into the grand scheme of things.

I've learned over the years it doesn't pay to whine and complain. Start adjusting and get on with your life. Remember the saying, "Laugh and the world laughs with you. Cry and you cry alone." I've learned to laugh at my circumstances. Someone who wears an eye patch can't afford to be too serious!

January 24

Kings

The best laid plans of kings have failed, where God has not. He is an all powerful, awesome God in whom we can depend and trust.
unknown

Your status here on earth has no bearing on whether or not you have eternal life in heaven. You'll have eternal life one place or the other so make plans accordingly. There will be kings, presidents, and other very important people who will be very surprised when they die. Some religions even bury their possessions with the deceased so they'll be able to use them on the other side.

If Jesus Christ is your Lord and Savior then you won't need anything from earth to go with you to paradise. Jesus is preparing a mansion for you with your name on it. Try to picture a perfect place waiting on you to arrive. All the joy, happiness, love, and peace that one could imagine, is in one wonderful place called heaven. All you have to do is ask Jesus Christ to be your master. So many people don't realize that Jesus is the door to heaven. He died on the cross because of your sins. He loved you that much! Now's your opportunity to love Him back.

January 25

Hope

Be of good courage, and He shall strengthen your heart, all ye that hope in the Lord.

Psalm 31:24

    Hope is a rare commodity in the secular world today. Tragedy after tragedy with the extreme weather, a rocky economy, outrageous gas prices with no relief in sight, layoffs, and rising food prices. The constant threat of terrorist attacks just adds to the doom and gloom. Where can you find hope in these circumstances? There is none. This is what non-believers have to deal with day in and day out. We Christians have to deal with the same problems, but we have hope of better things to come through our Lord. We know He will deliver us in our time of need. Who do the nonbelievers believe in? Themselves. Who do they call in time of need? Probably family and friends. I would rather have the Creator of the universe to call on. What about you? God created everything you see so why not call on the man at the top.

January 26

Refuge

The Lord also will be a refuge in times of trouble.
Psalm 9:9

What do you think of when you hear the word refuge? The dictionary says it's a shelter or protection from danger or distress or a means of resort for help in difficulty. When you're caught outside in a hailstorm you run for shelter, hopefully in a building. I was caught outside walking to class at Miss State when a tornado came over. I reached for the door handle on Hilburn Hall and I was lifted off my feet. It took several students to pull me to safety. Thank goodness they were there to help me.

I've been in eight car wrecks and it's always so comforting to see people coming to help. What if no one came?

Recently I saw a tape on the news where a man was struck by a car and no one came to help him. There were witnesses who called 911 for him, but no one stepped into the street to stop the on coming cars. That's so sad! What causes a person to stand by and not help someone in need? There has to be a total disconnect. You've heard of, "It's a dog eat dog world."

"Only the strong will survive" is another saying that is becoming more and more popular in today's world.

Where do you go for refuge?

January 27

Angels

Be not forgetful to entertain strangers: for thereby some have entertained angels unawares.

Hebrews 13:2

It's wonderful knowing that angels have been assigned to us for protection. If we could see them, we would be amazed at all that they do. I know I've worked my angels overtime. They have certainly earned their way.

Jesus is whispering to you right now, "Trust me." Why is that so hard for us? We use to leave our doors unlocked at night and drive with our cars unlocked. We wouldn't even consider that today. We are constantly on guard when we go anywhere. It pays to be vigilant, but you can't live in fear. Jesus doesn't want us to live that way. He wants us to totally trust Him. As Christians we need to pray for a shield of protection every time we head for the door.

Try to picture angels around you today.

January 28

Makeovers

And I will give them one heart, and I will put a new spirit within you; and I will take the stony heart out of their flesh, and will give them a heart of flesh.
That they may walk in my statutes and keep mine ordinances, and do them: And they shall be my people, and I will be their God.
Ezekiel 11:19-20

God uses some of the most unlikely people to call attention to the dramatic change He has made in their life. If He took a good person for example, there wouldn't be enough change for you to notice.

People don't like change and most will admit they need to change their life, but most refuse to give up what little control they think they have over their life. It's the fear of the unknown that keeps them locked in their sin. They have become comfortable in what they are doing. It's hard to break bad habits. It takes about 30 days to break a habit. It took me five attempts over a two-year period to stop smoking. I feel so much better now that I made that decision.

Whatever habits you have you will feel much better once the decision is made to improve yourself. God will help you.

He wants the best for you.

January 29

My Rock

He only is my rock and my salvation; He is my defense; I shall not be greatly moved.

Psalm 62:2

Before I became a mature Christian, I was influenced by people and things to stray from my values, but now that I've grown in the Lord, those things no longer can move me or have a hold on me. It's a shame that we don't have instant knowledge or strength when we become a Christian. Over time we grow and develop into the person God created us to be. It's important to remember that we are never fully there. There's always room to grow in the Christian faith until we take our last breath. Keep a check on yourself and make sure you are always moving forward.

January 30

My Defense

Because of His strength will I wait upon thee: for God is my defense.
Psalm 59:9

    I'm sure you've heard many times, "the one that is in me is stronger than the one in the world." I was told this too many times to count and it always made me feel better knowing God was with me. If you are feeling as if the world is against you, it is in a way. The world is mostly secular, so there are more people who would like to see you fail. That's why it's so important to surround yourself with brothers and sisters in Christ. We are united in Christ and can be a force to be reckoned with. We need to provide a united front against this evil world. United we stand. Divided we fall.

January 31

Praise

I will praise thee, O Lord, among the people: I will sing unto thee among the nations.

Psalm 57:9

    We have thousands of things to praise the Lord daily for, but do we really give Him credit? Sometimes we take credit for accomplishments when it was God at work. Have you given God credit for the beautiful sunrises and sunsets? Have you given God the credit for creating you? Have you given God the credit for the air that you breathe? What about the roof over your head, the food on your table, or your family?

    Most of the time people don't appreciate things until they lose them. God reminds us that if we don't use our talents, He'll take them away. God giveth and God taketh away. Remember that! Learn to give thanks daily. Also, don't be ashamed to thank God to your friends, family, and co-harts. It always touches my heart to hear people thank God for sparing their lives when they are standing in the middle of debris that use to be their home. That is a very powerful statement! Not many people can say that in such a tragic situation.

    What can you give praise for today?

February 1

Peace

For I know the thoughts that I think toward you, saith the Lord, thoughts of peace, and not of evil, to give you an expected end.
                                                                    Jeremiah 29:11

When we think of God and Jesus in heaven, we assume that they are very busy taking care of things. We don't really stop and think about them spending time thinking about us down here. This verse sets the record straight. They think about us. They pray about us, and they watch over us. How do we know? The bible tells us so. This verse states that they want peace for us. They are not sitting on the throne thinking of ways to punish us. Satan is the master of revenge and evil. Jesus and God are the masters of love.

When it says, "an expected end" that means to me they know from the beginning to the end what's going to happen. God knows what you are thinking and what you are going to do before you do. He knows what you're going to do tomorrow, today. Only you can control your thoughts. Sin starts with a thought. That's why it's so important to keep your mind pure.

February 2

Everlasting Life

For God so loved the world, that He gave His only begotten Son, that whosoever believeth in Him should not perish, but have everlasting life.

John 3:16

To me this is the most important verse in the Bible. I learned this verse as a child and it has been the foundation of my belief.

God loved us enough to send His Son to earth to live among us and then to give up His life so that our sins would be covered. Jesus took on all the sins of the world even though none were His. That's love in the purest form. Could you give up a child for the world to be saved? I know I couldn't have given up one of my girls.

So many people don't know you have to accept Jesus to get into heaven. Here's proof. You have to go through Jesus to get everlasting life. He was your sacrifice, not God. You have to accept God's Son if you want to live forever with Jesus and God in paradise. I pray I get to meet you there.

February 3

A True Friend

It doesn't matter where you go in life. It's whom you have beside you.
unknown

I was listening to James Merritt one day on TBN when I heard him say, "Every day should be Thanksgiving because even on my worst day, I know that God stands with me, God stands for me, and God stands beside me." This is so true. God goes everywhere you go and even though you can't see Him, He's there with you. That's awesome!

Sometimes I try to picture Jesus and God in my presence. We have an idea what Jesus looks like, but not a clue about God. God is a spirit. We'll have to wait till we are in heaven to see God for the first time.

I know people who are always dropping names of very important or famous people that they know. The only one that matters is Jesus Christ. Where salvation matters is whom you know and whom you believe in. Who is the most important person to you? Your life depends on it.

February 4

Rain Dance

Life isn't about waiting for the storm to pass. It's about learning to dance in the rain.

unknown

    I don't know where this saying came from. I found it in my notes, but thought it was important enough to share with you. There's a very important lesson in this saying.

    Some people completely shut down in a crisis, but this saying says we need to keep moving. There have been many crises in my life and when I look back over those troubled times, I did best when I kept putting one foot in front of the other, knowing that God would get me through yet another storm. He has never abandoned me, so why would He start now? God doesn't want us to suffer, but it happens. God whispers to us through the pain, but He yells at us through the storm. Learn to listen for Him. Some of my best moments with Jesus have been in the storm. I consider the storm a growing experience. Learn to dance in the rain. Without the storm, there would be no rainbows.

February 5

Be Not Afraid

In God have I put my trust: I will not be afraid what man can do unto me.

Psalm 56:11

We need to recite this verse every day before we head for the door. Fear keeps so many people from doing what they need to do for the Lord. Satan loves it.

Trust is not easy for so many people because of things done to them by others. This makes it very difficult for them to trust God. God is not going to make promises to you and then take them back. He means what He says. God can not lie to you. With God on your side, you should not be afraid. When God is for you then why worry about whom is not for you? God is all that matters.

I was a child who wanted to please everyone, but it's not possible to please everyone. I learned not to trust people that were very close to me for very good reasons. So I understand why people find it hard to trust anyone. You can trust God with your life.

February 6

My God

When I cry unto thee, then shall mine enemies turn back: this I know; for God is for me.

Psalm 56:9

I can not tell you how many times I have cried out for help from my God. He is the first one I call on. There is no one higher in authority. I go straight to the top. If anyone can handle your enemies for you, it's God Himself. Let God handle things for you. Put your troubles at the foot of the cross and walk away. God doesn't need your help. He can handle it all by Himself. In the past, I've tried to handle my own problems and failed miserably. If God can create the world in six days, then He can handle your problems in a snap. God doesn't give us what we can handle; God helps us handle what we are given. You are not weak because you can't fix your own problems. It's just better to hand your problems over to the almighty Father. Remember, Father knows best!

February 7

Appearances

The world sees what you do. God sees why you do it.

unknown

Recently I was criticized for doing foreign missions because a high school classmate thought I was over-looking the needy here at home. I immediately sat down to respond to her letter to inform her that home missions are at the top of our list. I don't know of a single person who works on foreign missions that hasn't started at home. If a person has a heart for helping the needy, they are not going to ignore someone right in front of them. God wants us to help all people who are in need. That means people who live in your community, your state, your country, and also around the world. I don't do charity because I know people are watching me. I help needy people because I know that's what God expects of me as a Christian. When we help people in need, they will see Christ through our actions and our love. We are Christ's hands and feet.

What will you do today for someone who is in need?

February 8

Whisper

Let us be silent that we may hear the whispers of God.
Ralph Waldo Emerson

We live very busy lives and it's hard to find a few silent moments in the day but we really need to make the time to listen for God. He speaks to us all the time but we're running around with our heads chopped off, ringing our hands, saying, "Woe is me!" How do you think that makes God feel? He has emotions, too.

Don't even try to reason away that there aren't enough minutes in the day! Who made the day and night? He did. If He can find the time to talk to you, then you need to listen. How do you feel when you are trying to tell someone something and they are ignoring you? It hurts! Stop hurting God and make time to listen.

February 9

Prison

The worst prison is a closed heart.

unknown

I've heard this saying many times in the course of my life. This is so true. What does a closed heart mean to you? To me it means someone has decided not to let anyone come into their life and refuses to allow themselves to love in the way that God meant when He designed the heart.

The heart is a muscle. A muscle grows with use. So a closed heart does not grow. That's not living to me. In a sense, that person is already dead.

You've heard love makes the world go round. I know love makes life a whole lot happier. Without love the world would seem so empty and useless and cold. Why choose that kind of life when you can have a life filled to overflowing with God at the center of your heart? I think a person with a closed heart doesn't love anyone including self. You must learn to love yourself before you can learn to love someone else. God is love!

Show someone some love today.

February 10

Blessed

The worst day with God is infinitely better than the best day with Satan.

unknown

    A friend of mine shared this saying with me. She carries it in her purse. Her family has been under attack by Satan for a year now. Her husband is recovering from colon cancer. No matter how bad you think you have it, there's always someone who has it worse. If we could just train ourselves to count our blessings and name them one by one, it would help.

    My husband just returned from a 10-day mission trip to Ghana, Africa to help with a leadership conference, build churches, and toured an orphanage. It really makes you feel blessed when you see how other people live. The villages are still very primitive and they do everything by hand. They cut their grass with machetes. It hurts my back just looking at the pictures.

    The people of Ghana are very friendly and really appreciate the help we bring. Medical clinics were set up to check blood pressure, eye infections, and worm treatments for the children.

    God instructs us to help the poor, needy, and widows. By getting out of our comfort zone, we are able to go where the need is great. We are to help anyone who needs it, home or abroad. If you aren't involved in charity, please give it a try. Be God's hands and feet.

February 11

Trust

Mine enemies would daily swallow me up: for they be many that fight against me, O thou most high.
What time I am afraid, I will trust in thee.

Psalm 56:2-3

I think we all have enemies. The more you work for the Lord, the more enemies you'll attract. There's no way everyone is going to love you and approve of all that you do. You have to develop thick skin in this world. Let what people say about you roll off your back, and keep your focus on Jesus Christ.

When I feel an evil presence, I demand that it leave using Jesus' name to make it flee. This is what the Bible instructs us to do. Try it.

Don't let fear consume you. He will protect you. Jesus is not a deadbeat father. He takes His job seriously.

February 12

Prayer Time

Evening, and morning, and at noon, will I pray, and cry aloud: and he shall hear my voice.

Psalm 55:17

Some people think that prayer time should be one brief designated time of day. Why limit it to a few minutes a day when you can spread your time with God out over the whole day? If you have a long commute, you can talk to God as you drive or sit in traffic. You can use your break time or lunchtime as well. If you understand how much God longs to spend some time with you, you would be more eager to find the time. He's a great listener. He's trust worthy and wouldn't reveal any of your secrets. You also don't have to make an appointment with Him. He's always there for you.

Spend some time with God today.

February 13

Heart Change

Jesus said our problems come from within. Change your heart from within.

Billy Graham

In my opinion, the heart is one of the most important organs in the body. If someone has an evil heart, then it really won't matter how smart he or she is. They will use their deceitful heart to hurt others and make life miserable for those around them. How does one develop a bad heart? It comes from abuse and it's usually deep-seated. Meaning the abuse goes way back into the childhood years. There are thousands of people in abusive situations as adults, also. It destroys a person's self-esteem.

How does a person begin to change a flawed heart? Ask Jesus, the healer, to heal the damage and help you to understand what happened and help you to forgive the person or persons that inflicted the abuse. It is possible to forgive even the worst offender. I'm living proof. I couldn't forgive on my own, but with the help of Jesus Christ, forgiveness was made possible. He'll do the same for you because it's what He wants all of us to do. Forgiveness is necessary for proper healing from the inside out.

Who do you need to forgive today?

February 14

Friendship

Two are better than one; because they have a good reward for their labor.
For if they fall, the one will lift up his fellow: but woe to him that is alone when he falleth; for he hath not another to help him up.
Ecclesiastes 4:9-10

This verse is meaning more and more to me, since I've been declared disabled. I have to rely on my friends to drive me places at night and my husband has to take off work to drive me to my doctor appointments in Memphis, TN. I'm very close to the limit of 20/50, which is the cutoff rate for driving. This is a very scary time for me because I've always been able to take care of myself or drive anywhere I want, whenever I want. I have only one eye, so this puts me in a dependable state. The sad thing is my husband is having vision problems, also. Our two daughters don't live close by so they aren't able to help. I feel for those who are blind and live alone.

Have there been times where you would like to find an isolated island and live in peace from the rest of the world? It would be nice for awhile, but I think you would eventually get lonely. God says it's better to have a friend to help when things get bad. Where two are in one accord in prayer, Jesus is there, also.

February 15

Season

To everything there is a season, and a time to every purpose under heaven.
A time to be born, and a time to die; a time to plant, and a time to pluck up that which is planted.

Ecclesiastes 3:1

My senior class voted this verse to be our class motto. I've always liked this verse. There is an order and a certain time for everything under heaven. God designed a very orderly universe.

We celebrate when a child is born and we cry when someone dies. It's hard to be happy for a loved one when they die, but if they are a Christian; we should be happy they've been called home. Heaven is our ultimate goal. We will catch up with them, eventually. I know when I see my mother again, I'll never be separated from her ever again. We will be joined in eternal time. Where we are going, there will be no knowledge of time. We won't have watches and clocks to watch.

I'm looking forward to the rapture. I see signs all around us with the extreme weather, wars and rumors of wars. Whenever it comes, you had better be ready. Unbelievers won't have a clue what's going on. Are you ready? Do you have friends that are not saved? Now is the time to secure your salvation, if it's not already sealed.

February 16

Understanding

Consider what I say; and the Lord give thee understanding in all things.

2 Timothy 2:7

I'm sure you've been in plenty of situations where you didn't understand why God allowed something to happen. Our brains are just not designed to think eternally. Americans use only 10% of their brains and that puts us at a disadvantage when it comes to understanding godly things. There are things that God didn't intend for us to understand and we'll have to wait till we get to heaven and ask God to explain. Some people believe we'll have instant knowledge when we enter the gates of heaven and others believe we'll spend eternity learning the answers. Either way, we'll get our questions answered.

I have to ask God to reveal to me what some verses mean. When I was a child, I had a very difficult time understanding the King James Version. Thank goodness I had great teachers who took the time to tell me what they thought God meant. Now I use different styles of Bibles to help me fully understand. You have to use discernment when talking or listening to others. You don't want to be misled by false prophets. Be on guard!

Ask God for discernment today.

February 17

Gift

Every good gift and every perfect gift is from above, and cometh down from the Father of lights, with whom is no variableness, neither shadow of turning.

James 1:17

When we think of gifts, we picture a beautifully wrapped package with a bow on top. Today, we're not talking about gifts we buy for others for special occasions. Those gifts aren't from God.

What do I consider a good gift from above? Being born into a good Christian family, marrying a godly man, living in a free country where you can worship freely, children, a roof over your head, food on the table, and lots of Christian brothers and sisters that add so much dimension to your life. I could go on and on but I would run out of space. How about you making your own list of gifts that God has blessed you with over the years? That's an exercise that will brighten any day.

February 18

Be Ready

But sanctify the Lord God in your hearts: and be ready always to give an answer to every man that asketh you a reason of the hope that is in you with meekness and fear.

1 Peter 3:15

As Christians it's our responsibility to be prepared when we are asked why we believe. Some may be seeking a new life and needs to hear from you why you have hope of a better life. Be careful how you answer, not coming off boastful, but with meekness and fear. Give a simple but straightforward answer so the seeker can easily understand. It's important to stress that God's grace is free and for everyone, no matter what they've done in the past. God loves everyone. God wants everyone to be saved and live with Him in paradise. Don't preach to others; just love them to Christ.

February 19

On High

Because He hath set his love upon me, therefore will I deliver Him: I will set Him on high, because He hath known my name.
He shall call upon me, and I will answer Him: I will deliver Him, and honour Him.
With long life will I satisfy Him and shew Him my salvation.
Psalm 91:14-16

The most powerful being in the history of the world knows your name. Not only does He know your name, but also He desires to answer your prayers and holds you in high regard. That's awesome. He's willing to rescue you from danger and see that you live out your numbered days. What more could you ask for? When you accept Jesus Christ as your savior, you become a member of a royal family with a king for a father. With that come expectations. You need to always present yourself as a Christian in every sense of the word. There are always people watching you. We are not to favor one select group of people or shun another. We are to love all people.

God expects us to obey Him and keep His commandments. Those are not optional, like some people believe. The way is narrow.

February 20

Saved

As for me, I will call upon God; and the Lord shall save me.
Psalm 55:16

Paul has made this vow to God and is determined not to let anything or anyone change his commitment to God. Paul believed that anyone who was sincere in heart could pray and ask Jesus into their hearts and they would be saved. Parents can't wish salvation for their children or anyone else. It's a personal decision for each and every soul.

It's so simple but it's so hard for people to accept. They think there has to be more to it, but it's not. God made it simple and free.

February 21

Suffering

Cast thy burdens upon the Lord, and He shall sustain thee: He shall never suffer the righteous to be moved.

Psalm 55:22

God is our judge, protector, healer, teacher, and anything else that you need. There's nothing too small or too big for Him to handle. Those that sin against you will be handled by the almighty God in God's time, not ours. That verse alone should make you sleep well at night. He's taking care of things while you are asleep.

Check yourself and see if there's anything you have not trusted to give to God. If so, what is holding you back? A large majority of people holds on to hurt feelings. There's no benefit to harboring a painful past. The time spent dealing with these feelings steals time away from our Lord. Time that could be used furthering the kingdom. Give your pain to God and forgive those who caused the damage. Then and only then can you properly move forward. You deserve a life free of painful memories.

February 22

Drink Daily

How about regular ladle dips into the well of God's grace? Drink deeply, my friend, and drink daily.

Max Lucado

In a world where prices of gas, food, and other needed items are constantly rising; it's refreshing to hear Max Lucado remind us to dip into God's well of grace. It's free and you can go there as often as you need to.

Since I'm steadily losing my vision, I purchased the Bible on CD, so I can save as much of my vision as possible. I don't want to strain the only eye that I have. Listening to Christian music is another way to dip into God's grace by surrounding yourself with inspiring music and not worldly music. Parents need to control what their children listen to. There's plenty of youthful Christian music to be bought for entertainment. Setting a good example is extremely important in raising children.

Are you a good influence or a bad influence?

February 23

Baptism

Therefore we are buried with Him by baptism into depth: that like as Christ was raised up from the dead by the glory of the Father, even so we also should walk in newness of life.

Romans 6:4

    When we have gone from unbelievers and been baptized, we have been reborn in spirit and are new creatures in Christ.

    Let me tell you about my baptism because people are still talking about it fifty years later. I had taken swimming lessons that summer so swimming was new to me. Our preacher was tall so more water than usual was used. Because we were short, a 2x4 board was placed across the bottom steps. The preacher reached out his hand to help us reach him and then he would place his hand over our nose and down we went. Well, he let go of me before I had a chance to get my feet back on the board and suddenly I found myself sinking. To keep from drowning, I started swimming for the other side, kicking my feet as hard as I could. The preacher got covered with water, but I was safe on the steps. I wasn't going to die while being baptized! The song leader saw me outside and he said he had one thing to say, "Your mother's money was spent well on swimming lessons!" I had to agree.

    Are you walking in newness?

February 24

Ask

If ye then, being evil, know how to give good gifts unto your children: How much more shall your heavenly father give the Holy Spirit to them that ask Him?

Luke 11:13

If you have not, it's because you have not asked. If I need something, I go to the Lord first. I've watched my daughters struggle with something, and I always ask them if they have prayed about it. Sometimes the answer is no and sometimes it is yes.

God probably gets tired of me asking over and over for one specific request but I'm not giving up on this one. It's an unspoken request that shall remain between the Lord and myself. Just recently, I've started seeing a change, so I know God is listening. He is at work on my request and even though I've prayed about this for years, I feel the end is coming. This is something I know God wants as much as I do. The prayers of a faithful wife are powerful!

February 25

Blessed

Blessed is the nation whose God is the Lord: and the people whom he hath chosen for his own inheritance.

Job 33:12

Christian men and women founded our country, but today Christianity represents only about 20% of our population. That's sad. During a survey about 90% acknowledged God exists but remember there are over 3,000 different deities. When someone says they believe in God, it might not be the God of the Bible.

Right now we have a Christian president, but my concern is someday that might not be the case. Will God remove His hand of protection if we don't keep a Christian in the White House? It's something to think about. It makes me sad to see how far America has gotten away from religion. How did we get in this shape? I pray Jesus comes back soon and takes us to paradise. I do feel blessed that I live in a free country because there are countries today that can't practice Christianity with in their borders. I'm praying that will change. Will you pray with me?

February 26

The Mouth

The mind of the righteous person thinks before answering...but the mouth of the wicked blurts out evil things.

Proverbs 15:28

Have you ever walked up to a stranger or sat down next to someone at a café and immediately you could tell that person was not a Christian? You don't even have to bring up religion. Their language removes all doubt. It hurts me to hear foul language and the young people today are using such horrible words that we never considered using coming up. My mom wouldn't even let us use the word darn.

If you use dirty or harsh words, you are speaking evil to the air. Who controls the air? Satan. Don't work for Satan. Instead use encouraging words that build up and inspire people to do great things.

I cringe when I hear a parent tell their child they are stupid. These are damaging words. I wasn't told that as a child and I never talked to my girls that way. I never talked to my students that way, either. We need to enforce the law that says we are not to cuss in public.

February 27

Put Down

Cross insecurity-putting others down.

unknown

I saw this saying and thought it was interesting. People who are not secure in their faith may not fully realize just how important they are to Christ. If they did, they wouldn't have an inferiority complex. People who are insecure will say things to bring others down to their level. I know a few people who fit this description.

If you are a Christian and you know Christ died for you; then you should not be a part of this type of behavior. Jesus Christ loved you enough to die on the cross just for you. You are that important to Him. If you were the only living person left on this earth, Jesus would have still died on the cross just for you.

So next time someone puts you down, rise above it. I tell them, I'm so sorry they feel that way, but I'll be sure and put them at the top of my pray list. The look on their face is priceless!

February 28

Promise

God didn't promise days without pain,
laughter without sorrow,
nor sun without rain,
but He did promise strength for the day,
comfort for the tears,
light for the way.

unknown

God doesn't promise us a safe journey but a safe landing. In the Bible it tells us we will have trials and tribulations. I don't know anyone who has lived a long life without any troubles. It's just not possible. My comfort during those tribulations is that I wasn't going through them alone. I felt God's presence every time.

When we had to hospitalize our oldest daughter with an eating disorder, there were some terrible things said to us by family members. You would expect it from others, but not from your own family. If you can't be supportive in a time of need, keep your mouth shut. I had to learn to stay focused on our daughter and forget the hateful remarks. I turned these people over to God to deal with them. He will take care of it for you. Remember that He is the judge and jury! Amen!

February 29

Storm

Sometimes God calms the storm...sometimes He lets the storm rage and calms His child.

unknown

One of my favorite stories in the Bible was when Jesus was asleep and a storm was threatening to turn over the boat. The disciples were scared to death. They woke Jesus and asked Him for help. All Jesus had to do was speak to the storm and it stopped. I would have loved to have seen the faces of the disciples. I'm sure they were in shock. I don't think they really understood how powerful Jesus really was. Wouldn't you like to have a friend like that? You can for the asking.

March 1

Heaven

Our homeland is in heaven.

Philippians 3:20

Earth is not your real home. When you die, you will spend eternity one place or the other, smoking or non-smoking?

I've been saved since I was nine years old and it's comforting to know that when I take my last breath, the next breath will be in heaven.

If you haven't read <u>Heaven Your Real Home</u> by Joni Eareckson Tada, I suggest you read it. I love that book! Even as a child I loved hearing about heaven. I know I asked my mother a thousand questions about heaven. I'm glad I did because when she died, I had a better understanding of where she was. She knew she was dying and she wasn't scared because she knew where she was going. She was an example to people on how to die with dignity. I thank God for having an amazing Christian mother. I know for sure, she'll meet me at the gate when it's my time to leave this earth. I can't wait!

March 2

The Kingdom

Flesh and blood can not have a part in the kingdom of God. Something that will ruin cannot have a part in something that never ruins.
1 Corinthians 15:50

When we die, we will be given glorified bodies. Amen! This body that I have now has been glued back together so many times. I'm only 59 but my body is like that of a 90 yr. old with three different kinds of arthritis, degenerative disk disease, congestive heart disease, failing vision, osteoporosis, and high blood pressure. So I can't wait to see what our glorified bodies will be like. It has to be out-of-this-world, because it can't decay. No more aches and pain. No need for sleep. No need for food or water and no need for exercise. Amen and Amen! That's the best news I've heard in quite a while. Have we got the best designer and creator or what?

Another good book I want you to read is <u>90 Minutes in Heaven</u> by Don Piper. My favorite chapter is the third one about the gate and what he saw when he stepped into heaven.

He didn't get very far before he was sent back to his mangled body. Don said he was singing a song and suddenly he was back in his car singing the same song with the preacher, who had stopped to pray over his body. He had been dead for 90 minutes so you can imagine the shock of the preacher and the policemen on the scene. What a miracle!

March 3

The Race

Wherefore seeing we also are compassed about with so great a cloud of witnesses, let us lay aside every weight, and the sin which doth so easily beset us, and let us run with patience the race that is set before us.
Hebrews 12:1

If you've ever run track, you'll know how disciplined you have to be when you are competing in a race. Our relay team messed up from time to time because our timing was off or we dropped the baton. One time I was changing hands and accidentally hit my hip with the baton and it went flying off the track disqualifying us. From then on I made sure I had a firm grip on the baton. That was so embarrassing.

Life is the same way. We let things distract us and sometimes we end up off the path. We need to be vigilant by keeping our eyes on Jesus.

I know God doesn't operate on our schedule. This is where trust comes into play. In His time, not ours!

March 4

My Voice

I cried unto the Lord with my voice; with my voice unto the Lord did I make my supplication.

Psalm 142:1

    I read somewhere that we are mud on the bottom of our enemies' boots until we learn to come to God for his help. We can do nothing apart from God.
    David made this cry while he was hiding in a cave. David knew who could save him. David laid his troubles before the Lord and didn't hold anything back. David had a heart for God and God loved him dearly. It showed.
    Next time you've got your back against the wall, do what David did and cry out to the Lord for help. He's waiting to hear from you.

March 5

The Throne

Looking unto Jesus the author and finisher of our faith; who for the joy that was sent before him endured the cross, despising the shame, and is set down at the right hand of the throne of God.

Hebrews 12:2

Jesus left the comforts of heaven to come to earth as a baby. I can't help but wonder at what age did He realize that He was different from the others. I know at 12, He was discussing the meaning of verses with the elders of the church. He started His ministry at 30 yrs. of age and by 33 He was hung on the cross.

Have you ever wondered how He felt when His own people turned against Him? People called Him crazy.

When my family turned against me for going public about my abuse, I had an idea what Jesus must have felt. I was also called crazy. I was called a liar when I have told nothing but the truth. I also prayed the prayer that Jesus prayed on the cross, "Father please forgive them for they know not what they do." I asked God to forgive my siblings. They still don't have a clue what damage they have done. If this has happened to you, there's only one thing to do. Turn them over to God and ask God to help you forgive those that have harmed you. God will be more than happy to take care of it for you.

March 6

Sacrifice

No matter that your background or religion, Christ died for you.
unknown

Christianity is the only religion where someone has died for you so your sins would be forgiven. Jesus became our sacrifice. The only innocent man to ever walk the face of this earth died for you.

As a child, I didn't understand why Jesus didn't come down off the cross. I knew He had the power to come down. Jesus willingly stayed on the cross because of His love for you and me. That's amazing love! Is there anyone you know today that loves you enough to die for you? I don't know of anyone. I think my mother would have died for me. I know I would die for my girls. I've lived a full life and I'm ready to go home. Are you ready? You better get ready because one day will be your last.

March 7

Savior

Jesus Christ-equal opportunity savior.

unknown

Jesus traveled with a select group during His ministry, but His message was for everyone. The disciples were handpicked for a reason. They were an odd group but they had a divine purpose. This tells me that God can use anyone. Even the lowest on the ladder of jobs can be used.

We are very careful in the work force to make things fair when hiring people, but I know there are still companies not complying with the equal opportunity laws. Well, you don't have to worry when it comes to salvation. Jesus doesn't have a checklist when you come to Him. Salvation is free and is available to those who are sincere in their asking.

March 8

Of God

Ye are of God, little children, and have overcome them: because greater is he that is in you than He that is in the world.

1 John 4:4

I heard this verse over and over through out my adult life. When you accept Jesus Christ as your savior, He sends the Holy Spirit to come live in your heart. As a child we don't understand this but as we grow in Christ, we become more and more confident that Christ is really with us in everything we do and everywhere we go. As a child, I was scared of the dark, but over time I've gotten use to it. Now that my vision is very limited, it's good that I'm no longer scared of the dark. I lost my left eye to a very rare tumor that doctors tell me I was born with. It's possible that as a child, I was scared of the dark because I wasn't able to see as well in the dark. I really noticed it when I started driving and many times my most difficult moments were at night seeing driveways and turns. Now I'm not allowed to drive at night anymore. Am I scared of going blind? No, because I know God will provide for me. God is greater than any problem.

March 9

Counsel

I will instruct you and teach you in the way which you should go; I will counsel you with my eye upon you.

Psalm 32:8

Are you teachable? If you have trouble following instruction and answering to a high authority then you will have a great deal of trouble following God's will for your life.

We're all born with a purpose. Have you discovered your purpose according to God's plan for your life? If not, ask God to reveal His purpose to you.

To follow God's will, you have to die to self so His work can be done. This world does not revolve around us like most believe. It's all about Him. He created the earth and He is in control of everything. You are either working for Christ or against Him.

March 10

Nearer

Draw near to God and He will draw near to you.

James 4:8

How close are you to God? Do you want to be closer? What is keeping you from being closer? If there is something blocking the way, then it's up to you to remove the barrier. God doesn't put up walls. God wants to be closer to you. He loves you with His whole heart. Do you love God with your whole heart?

I was mad at God when He didn't heal my mother and she died of breast cancer at age 50. I didn't understand why He needed her more than I did. I was 16 yrs. old. I had to learn to trust God because I know He knows what's best for me. God doesn't make mistakes. Now that I'm older and wiser, I realize my mother is better off in heaven than if she had remained here on earth. Her time was up. My mother made a life long impression on so many people, not just her children. She was a great example of what a Christian is suppose to be.

When you're gone from this earth, will people say good things about you? Are you leaving a legacy?

March 11

Fearless

Do not fear, for I am with you.

Isaiah 41:10

    This verse is extremely difficult to follow, because there are so many things that scare us, especially in today's times when we have terrorists threatening us every time we turn around.

    When I was a child, the schools made us get under our desks to practice an attack from a nuclear bomb. I don't think they do that anymore. When I was teaching, we practiced tornado and fire drills.

    When I became a parent, I lived in fear of something happening to my children. Now that I know they are saved, I don't live in fear because I know where they're going after this life. Death is all around us, but as Christians we are not to fear death. I feared death as a child because I experienced it at a very early age. The thought of never seeing loved ones again on this earth scared me to death. It was so final!

    Now, that I'm much older, I welcome death because I know of a better place and a better life beyond. I can't wait to lock eyes with Jesus for the very first time.

March 12

Help

God is our refuge and strength, a very present help in trouble.
Psalm 46:1

What's the very first thing you do in a time of trouble? I recently had to call 911 with severe chest pains. I had difficulty breathing and wasn't sure if I was having a heart attack or not. I decided to call and let the EMTs decide what was going on. It's better to err on the side of caution. I spent a week in the hospital because my blood pressure medicine was too high and I was dehydrated. I spent a lot of time in prayer. I was hooked up to too many tubes to do anything else. I got to meet some nurses that I've never met before and I live in a very small town. Our paths crossed for a reason. While talking to one nurse, she was asking me about the experience and I told her, I thought this was it. She asked if I was scared of dying. I told her I had made my peace with God and I was ready to go home.

March 13

Promise

I will never forsake you.

Deuteronomy 4:31

The Bible is full of promises, but I think this one is very important. A large number of people have been abandoned at some time or another in their life. It's most damaging when it happens to a child. This action alone causes problems well into adulthood.

People who have been abandoned will have the most difficulty believing that God will never forsake them. There's probably nothing you can say to help them. They will learn on their own over time that God is still there.

This Bible verse is a good one to post on your mirror so you can read it every day as you get dressed for work. It's worth speaking it out loud daily.

March 14

Caring

Casting all your care upon Him; for He careth for you.
1 Peter 5:7

Here's proof that God really does care for you. There's no chance of a rejection because He loves you so much. He loves you more than anyone you know. If you think no one loves you, you're wrong. There's one that loves you so. He's not just anyone, either. He's the master of everything. He's brilliant, He's powerful, He's divine, and He's the man at the top. He's yours for the asking.

March 15

Rest

Blessed is the man whom thou chastenest, O Lord, and teachest him out of thy law; that thou mayest give him rest from the days of adversity, until the pit be digged for the wicked for the Lord will not cast off His people, neither will He forsake His inheritance.

Psalm 94:12-14

This pretty much says it all. We are blessed! You may not feel blessed at this reading, but if you make a list of what you're thankful for, I think you will come to the conclusion that you are blessed beyond any doubt. Even if your list was, I have a pulse; then you are blessed. Because if you don't have a pulse then you are dead!

March 16

Misuse

"If you don't understand, you'll misuse it and you'll abuse it."
Rick Warren

Rick Warren wrote, <u>The Purpose Driven Life</u>. I knew what my purpose was before I read his book, but what it did was confirm what I thought my purpose really was. I had been asking God for years to reveal to me His purpose and He did just that. God wants you to know His plans for you, so He'll help you figure it out. Just be sure you're a good listener. Some people like to do all the talking. You must learn to be still and be silent.

Sometimes it's necessary to read a scripture from different styles of Bibles and there are commentaries to help you understand what God is trying to tell you. It's no use, if you don't understand.

March 17

Snowstorm

"Sometimes God throws us into a spiritual snowstorm, so we can focus on Him."

Dr. David Jeremiah

I listen to Dr. Jeremiah when I have the chance. I like his style of preaching and he includes personal stories. Dr. Jeremiah is very passionate and it keeps your attention. Preachers are not immune to tragedy. Dr. Jeremiah has talked often about the child that they lost. He has also battled cancer.

What is a spiritual snowstorm? First, you need to understand what happens during a snowstorm. You can very easily lose your way. Snow can fall so fast, that you experience a whiteout. Everything is white in all directions and you lose your bearings. You suddenly don't know your north from your south and etc. Add the spiritual component and you become confused on which way you think God wants you to go. I have a friend right now taking time off from the ministry because He doesn't know what God wants him to do next. Sometimes the answer doesn't come quickly. Learn to be still and know that he is God.

March 18

Perfect

Make you perfect in every good work to do His will, working in you that which is well pleasing in His spirit, through Jesus Christ; to whom be glory forever and ever.
Amen.

Hebrews 13:21

We as humans are far from perfect but through Christ we can work perfectly through Him. I'm disabled and can't work for myself, but that doesn't mean I can't work for the Lord. There are things I can do perfectly for Him without ever leaving my home. The power of the word is mighty. With pen in hand, I write about my love for my Master. I share my experiences with those that are still suffering and let them know He can heal them, also. Stop wasting time for the end is near. There are souls to be saved!

March 19

Assurance

Let your conversion be without covetousness; and be content with such things as ye have: for he hath said, "I will never leave thee, nor forsake thee."

Hebrews 13:5

By now, I guess you've noticed there are many verses in the Bible that says, "I will never leave thee, not forsake thee." There's a reason for that. Sometimes we have to hear important messages over and over before we believe them. God is driving this one home. He's not pulling your leg or trying to trick you. God is holy and He can't be a part of deception. God is truth!

March 20

Grace

Let us therefore come boldly unto the throne of grace, that we may obtain mercy, and find grace to help in time of need.
Hebrews 4:16

God never gets upset when we come to Him with a need. He gets upset when we don't come to Him. He's waiting for you to ask Him for help. What are you waiting for? An invitation?

God has mercy and grace that He wants to bestow upon you. That's worth saying again. He's the only one!

March 21

The Mark

I press toward the mark of the prize of the high calling of God in Christ Jesus.

Philippians 3:14

I know if you've set goals before, you know about striving toward the finish. After all your hard work when you've finally completed your goal, it's an amazing sense of accomplishment. You feel so much better about yourself because you stuck to your plans.

If you've ever tried to diet and couldn't stay with the program, you feel like a failure.

Here's a goal that anyone can achieve. Put your focus on Jesus at the end of the race of life and don't let Satan distract you.

March 22

Service

Wherefore we receiving a kingdom which cannot be moved, let us have grace, whereby we may serve God acceptably with reverence and godly fear. For our God is a consuming fire.

Hebrews 12:28-29

How important is it to you to know that heaven can not be moved? The more I hear about nuclear bombs being manufactured, the more I appreciate a heaven that is indestructible. Our temporary home can be destroyed. When I was young, I was told that the first nuclear bomb would set off a chain reaction around the world. Just seven nuclear bombs spaced around the earth could cause an explosion that could blow up the world. Thank goodness our real home is not under threat. Amen!

March 23

Everything Lost

Faith that has not been tested, is faith that can not be trusted.
unknown

    I love reading church signs. This saying was on a church sign in Senatobia, MS. What better way to get a message to the general public than posting it on the highway for all to see? My faith has been tested over and over so I know my faith works. It's so comforting to me to know that my God has my best interest at heart. He's not too busy to handle my needs. I love that about Him. You don't have to wait for Him to get home from work or finish doing something. He is at your beckoning call.
    Will you call on Him today?

March 24

The Upright

The upright shall dwell in your presence.

Psalm 140:14 (NKJV)

You don't have to wait for eternity to enjoy God's presence now. You can train yourself to think eternally. Look at this world as a pass through. That doesn't mean to sit back with folded arms. There's always something that needs to be done for our Lord, however small. When you do things for those who can't help themselves, you are letting them see Christ through you. Be sure not to take the credit for yourself, but give all the glory to God.

Take an account of yourself. Remember character is whom you are when no one is looking. Don't do things just to get your picture in the newspaper. Remember who is watching.

March 25

Goodness

Surely goodness and mercy shall follow me all the days of my life; and I will dwell in the house of the Lord forever.
                                                            Psalm 23:6(NKJV)

I love this verse. I learned it as a child and it has served me well over the years. No matter what I've gone through, God has always watched over me and carried me through my storms. Think back over your most defining moments in life and have you not come out the other side wiser and stronger for the experience? Why does God allow these trails and tribulations? You'll have to ask God that one when you get to heaven.

We aren't expected to know why in every situation. I asked myself why God allowed me to hit a woman in the street in front of my car. I asked if He was trying to teach me a lesson or was He trying to tell me I needed to stop driving. I never got an answer on that one. I know my driving days are numbered. I would rather give up my driving than hurt another person. I care more about others than my independence. Remember that whatever you have lost here, you'll be perfect in heaven. I'll have two eyes for eternity.

March 26

Love

He ...loads me with love and mercy.

Psalm 103:4

About two years ago I asked my mother's helper if there was anything that I had done to cause my siblings to treat me so badly. Mott informed me that she was there the day my mother told my siblings that she was expecting another child. Mott said that she had never witnessed anything like that reaction before. So even before I was born, I was not wanted by my own siblings. Children can be very perceptive about feelings especially when they are not loved. Thank goodness, I received a lot of love from my mother, my aunts and uncles, and my grandparents.

I learned very early how much Jesus loves me. That was the very first song that my mother taught me. I sang it over and over according to my Aunt Catherine, for whom I am named. Jesus' love has filled a void that nothing else can fill. Some people turn to drugs, alcohol and sex to fulfill that need. No heart can be satisfied until God fills it first. Jesus and God love you more than the world!

March 27

Christ

In Christ there is all of God in a human body.
Colossians 2:9 (TLB)

I read this verse the other day and realized it's the first time I've ever read this verse. I've made several attempts to read the Bible all the way through, but have yet to finish this task. My husband has read the Bible all the way through five times. I'm currently listening to the Bible on CD so this time I feel confident in finally hearing all of the Bible. It makes you wonder what you've been missing. I like discovering new verses. Even though, I've never read this verse, it's something that I've always known. Jesus was half man and half God. He could feel all the emotions that we feel. He felt hunger, thirst, pain and suffering just like you and me. He possessed the powers of God. That's why He was able to perform miracles. Why didn't the people of His day believe He was who He was? They were there to see the miracles first hand and still didn't believe. I know some people today that wouldn't have believed even if they had been present. That's so sad to me. We still need to witness to all people.

March 28

Believe

If you believe, you will get anything you ask for in prayer.
Matthew 21:24

One thing that has helped me is a prayer journal. I write down the name, date and need. When that prayer is answered, I write down the results and date. This is a very good way to see that God really does answer prayers. It may take a while, sometimes even years, but you still need to see that God answers prayers in His time; not ours.

God knows our needs before we even ask, but it's still important that you come to God in prayer and state your requests. It's very important that you believe that God will help you and He wants what's best for you.

God always answers your prayers, but sometimes it may be no instead of yes. Did you always get a yes when you asked your parents for something? I know the answer to that one. No parent has always said yes to their children. I know some that have come close. Look closely at their children. How did the children turn out? When they grow up, life isn't going to cater to their wishes. They will struggle and not get along with others. It's an injustice to raise children that way. God is not going to be an injustice to you.

March 29

Works

I work and struggle, using Christ's great strength that works so powerfully in me.

Colossians 1:29

As Christians we are given special strengths through the Holy Spirit that lives within us. Some use these strengths while others do not.

While working an Emmaus Walk, I was asked to go pray over a sick young man in one of the cabins. I grabbed my anointing oil and headed for the door. I had only anointed a sick friend prior to this experience so I felt a little inexperienced in this area, but I was willing to go in the Lord's name. As I was walking to the cabin, I prayed for God to use me to help this young man. I was willing to go in His name and God did the rest. I placed the oil on his forehead and asked in Jesus' name that He be healed. Within the hour, this young man was able to return to the conference room and enjoy the rest of the day and night. It was God's will that this man be healed. I believed and the young man believed that God could and would heal him. Our prayers were answered.

March 30

Blessed Assurance

Don't have insurance? I have blessed assurance.

unknown

    You have probably heard the hymn, "Blessed Assurance". I have sung it too many times to count. It says, "Blessed assurance Jesus is mine." I've known Jesus is mine since I was nine years old. He'll always be mine. I have the blessed assurance that I'll be spending eternity with Him. What better insurance is there?

    The insurance that we carry on our cars, homes, and property has little fine print and clauses that we don't sometimes understand. With Jesus there is no fine print or clauses that we don't understand. Salvation is very simply stated in John 3:16. You can't get any simpler than that. There's no deception here. Learn to trust Jesus.

March 31

Cross

Not Blue Cross but old rugged cross.

unknown

When I was in children's choir, I was asked to sing, "The Old Rugged Cross" at our recital for our parents. Mrs. McElroy had me sing the song like I first learned it and then I sang it over like she had taught me. There was a remarkable difference. It's still one of my favorite songs.

It called the old rugged cross, the emblem of suffering and shame. It's where Jesus laid down His life for your sins. It says we'll exchange it soon day for a crown. I think we'll then lay our crowns at the feet of Jesus. After all it's all about Him. Next time you see a cross, think on these things.

April 1

Blessed

Blessed is the man who finds wisdom, the man who gains understanding.

Proverbs 3:13

I don't know how many times wisdom or understanding is mentioned in the Bible but my concordance has 234 listings for wisdom, 247 for wise and 14 listings for wisely. Understand has 91, understandest list 4, understandeth has 11, understanding has 160 while understood has 37 listings. This gives you an idea how important these words are to God.

You can read God's word every day, but it won't help if you don't understand it so you can apply it. The more we understand the better we'll be able to explain it to someone else. Bible study will give you a better picture of what God is trying to tell you. It also gives you an opportunity to discuss the different interpretations people might have. I have thoroughly enjoyed Beth Moore's studies because she has a woman's perspective on things. She makes you think in ways you've never experienced before. It's refreshing.

April 2

Love

Be very diligent to love the Lord your God for your own well being.
Joshua 23:11

It was the love of God that kept me safe in a chaotic world. They say love makes the world go round. It certainly helps one get through each day. But we're not talking about the love between a man and a woman. We're talking about loving God. He warns us about loving this world. If you love this world more than Him, then you won't be spending eternity with Him in heaven.

God says if we love Him, we'll keep His commandments. This would be a good time to review the commandments to see how well you are doing. There may be something you need to work on. I believe there's always room for improvement as long as we have breath in us. We should be constantly striving to be more like Christ.

What can you do today to get closer to Christ?

April 3

Sinless

For we do not have a high priest who is unable to sympathize with our weaknesses, but One who has been tested in every way as we are, yet without sin.

Hebrews 4:15

Jesus was the only one to ever walk on this earth without sin. He was perfect in every way. Does He expect us to be perfect? No, way. We are humans who will make mistakes. Thank goodness, God erases our mistakes. He is also a God of second chances.

Does God understand why we fail? Of course, He does. Jesus felt all the emotions, love and suffering that we experience even today. Most people may not know your weaknesses, but He knows them all. Does He look at us any differently because He knows all? I don't think so. He loves us despite our weaknesses. He loves us no matter what we've done in the past. Ask for forgiveness and your sins are wiped out forever. Amen!

April 4

Agape

We have come to know and to believe the love that God has for us. God is love, and the One who remains in love remains in God, and God remains in him.

1 John 4:16

In the dictionary it says that agape means wide open, being in a state of wonder, love, and love feast. In the Bible it says that God is love which is called agape.

It's hard for us to know the extent of God's love since we have never met Him face to face. This is where trust comes in to play. If you have trouble trusting people, this makes it even more difficult for you to believe that God loves you this much. He really does love you. You are the apple of His eye. Wrap your arms around yourself and give yourself a hug from God. The experts say we need five hugs a day to feel really loved. You are loved by God, whether you like it or not!

Show some love to someone today.

April 5

Transformed

Do not be conformed to this age, but be transformed by the renewing of your mind, so that you may discern what is the goods pleasing, and perfect will of God.

Romans 12:2

Have you noticed that each generation embraces more and more of the world? What one generation tolerates the next embraces. This trend is very disturbing. Satan is stealing our children.

Usually what we want is not God's will for us. That's why we need to renew our minds, so that we can become more like Christ. God can't think the evil thoughts we have. We need to guard our souls to keep these thoughts under control. The Holy Spirit will help you achieve this goal. A sin starts with a thought and then it's applied to action. If you can control your mind with the help of the Holy Spirit, then you're closer to God than most. God loves obedient children.

Will you change for God?

April 6

Peace

If only you had paid attention to my commands then your peace would have been like a river, and your righteousness like the waves of the sea.

Isaiah 48:18

If only we had paid attention. Hello! Sometimes we need to be hit between the eyes with a 2x4. Trust me, it's easier just to follow the commands and you'll be rewarded for being obedient. God adores obedient children. You know how important it is to have obedient children. An unruly child can turn your life upside down and inside out.

God promises you peace like a river and righteousness like the waves of the sea, which means plentiful and always coming. Waves never stop. That's the kind of peace we all need in this wicked world. You can't buy it. It doesn't come in a glass or in a pill form. Only true peace comes from God.

Ask God today to grant you unending peace like a river.

April 7

Contentment

I don't say this out of need, for I have learned to be content in whatever circumstances I am.

Philippians 4:11

How many content friends do you have? They are a rare breed. This is a must have society where neighbors try to keep up with others. This is insane. We should be thankful for what we have. Compared to the state of the world, we have it made here in the United States. We have running water, electricity, grocery stores, and etc.

My husband just returned from Ghana. The pictures of the villages are very primitive and will make you appreciate what you have, if nothing else. I can't take the heat because of my congestive heart disease and when my electricity goes off, I'm very uncomfortable. I thank God for the good roof over my head and for the food on my table. I live a very blessed life compared to most. My husband and I are at a point where we can share with those who are in need. Our heart goes out to those less fortunate. I can credit my mom for teaching me to share. It's what Jesus instructs us to do in His name.

What will you share with someone today?

April 8

The Test

The Lord your God is testing you to know whether you love the Lord your God with all your heart and all your soul.
Deuteronomy 13:3

We are tested from time to time about our loyalty. Take a good long look at Job. Did he deserve what happened to him? God allowed Satan to have his way with him to prove Job's love for God. Job passed the test with flying colors. If you were allowed to lose everything you owned, including your children, how would you have made it? People are constantly losing everything through hurricanes, floods, earthquakes, fires, and tornadoes. It's hard but they learn to pick up the pieces and move forward with the help of our Lord and Savior. God eases the pain and makes it possible to continue. God restored Job two times over what he lost for his loyalty. Job loved God with all his heart and all his soul and it showed.

I pray I never have to experience losing everything. I've lost enough health wise. I don't want pity because I lost an eye and have failing vision in the other eye. I believe everything happens for a reason.

Will you pass the next test?

April 9

The Best

And we know that all things work together for the good to them that love God, to them who are called according to His purpose.
Romans 8:28

    I chose this verse for my birthday because it's my favorite verse in the Bible. It was my Grandpa Simpson's favorite verse and also my Uncle Arnold's favorite. This verse assures us that God is in control and He will turn every thing to good no matter what happens to us as long as we are in His will and it's in His plan.

    Look at Joni Eareckson Tada for example. She broke her neck diving at age 19. Joni has spent her whole adult life in a wheelchair. She could have become a very angry woman, but instead she chose to serve the Lord. She has written countless books, given countless talks, and has painted beautiful pictures with a paintbrush held with her teeth. This woman is amazing! God has used her in a mighty way. Had Joni not had the accident, I'm not sure she would have accomplished the things she's known around the world for today. Millions know her name. See what God can do with a willing heart!

    What are you willing to do for God today?

April 10

Follow

I am the light of the world; he that followeth me shall not walk in darkness, but shall have the light of life.

John 8:12

    We live in a very dark world, but if you walk in Christ, He will light your path. I have no idea how unbelievers handle the ways of the world. What hope could they possibly have if they don't have Christ as their Savior? Can you remember a time before you were saved where all seemed lost in your life? Now we have a promise of a better tomorrow. What do unbelievers have to look forward to after they have left this earth? I've heard famous people say that they believe we cease to exist when we die. I've got news for them. They will live eternally one place or the other. So many people will be shocked when they draw their last breath. I'm thankful I was raised in a Christian home.

    What are you thankful for today?

April 11

Seek

Ask, and it shall be given you; seek, and ye shall find; knock, and it shall be opened unto you.

Matthew 7:7

People think this verse gives them free range to ask and receive whatever they desire. This is not what God had in mind. Be careful what you ask for. I've learned to seek God's will, not mine. God knows what I need even when I don't. This world is not about me. It's not about you, either. When you are living in God's will, He will open doors and opportunities for you that never even entered your mind. I never had a plan to help people in Africa and now my husband and I are raising money to build churches in Ghana. God sends people into your life for a reason. If you're not open to God's will, you'll miss those opportunities.

Are you seeking God's will?

April 12

Shout

Then shalt thou call, and the Lord shall answer; thou shalt cry, and He shall say, "Here I am."
Isaiah 58:9

When I read this verse, I'm reminded of my only trip to ICU. There's a place no body wants to go! I had surgery to remove a tumor that was found behind my left eye. I'll spare you the details of the surgery, but it took almost 12 hours to complete the removal. I was in my third day in ICU when I reached my all time low. I blew out my IV and the tech was in the process of redoing it. He was crying and I was crying. I cried out to the Lord and I felt Him enter the room. He laid down on the table with me and covered my legs with His clothing. When I shared my story with a friend, they wanted to know what pain medication I was given. I wasn't given anything. My IV wasn't even hooked up. I went to sleep and when I woke up they were rolling me to my room. Without the life threatening experience, I wouldn't have experienced the most precious moment with Jesus to date. I don't wish any life threatening moments for you, but I do wish you'd learn to cry out to our Father in your time of need. You'll be amazed at what He'll do for you. He loves you so much!

Have you talked to Him today?

April 13

Training

Train up a child in the way he should go: and when he is old, he will not depart from it.

Proverbs 22:6

I can not thank God enough for teaching me how important it was to raise my children in the church. I didn't have any help from my husband, which made it really hard for me to get to church in one piece. I was raised in the church and I remembered how happy I was to learn about Jesus. I wouldn't have handled things as well as I did in my childhood, had I not had the foundation that my mother insisted we have. You had to be on your deathbed to miss church. I never had perfect attendance, but I could count on one hand the number of times I missed.

I was taught Bible verses that remained with me through out my life. I was taught to fear the Lord and respect Him. If a child is not taught by the age of ten to respect authority, when they reach their teenage years, they will not respect and obey our laws; much less God's laws. It's extremely difficult to reason with an adult who has been allowed to go his or her own way with no supervision. The prisons are full of them.

April 14

Creator

Every house is builded by some man; but he that built all things is God.

Hebrews 3:4

We've come along way, baby when it comes to technology. We pat ourselves on our backs and think we are so smart, but who deserves the credit? Who created us? None other than God Himself. Look at the complex human body and you know without a doubt that we did not develop from apes. I have to laugh at the science shows that try to explain how we got here. They need to put those smart brains into finding us another source of energy. Big Bang Theory! Give me a break! Everything you see came from God! We can't take credit for any designs here on earth. Give God credit for His divine plan.

April 15

Light

For thou wilt light my candle: the Lord my God will enlighten my darkness.

Psalm 18:28

If you will turn your life over to God, He will take care of everything for you. He loves details! His hands are tied until you give Him permission to take over. What's holding you back? Afraid to give up control? Who are you fooling? You don't have control anyway! Hello! You have free will to choose your path, but you don't have control over what happens to you.

Get on the same page with Christ. If you're not working with Him, then you're working against Him. If you allow yourself to speak negatives to the air, who is your master? It's not God! You can't serve both for you'll love one and hate the other. I chose to serve my Lord.

Whom will you serve today?

April 16

Broken Heart

The Lord is nigh unto them that are of a broken heart.
Psalm 34:18

    I think everyone has had their heart broken at some time in their life. I had my heart broken three months after my mother died and it took me a very long time to get over it. I think it was my inability to cope with my mother's death that drove my boyfriend away. I was inconsolable like Job. The pain was indescribable. Some people say it's like having your heart dung out with a spoon. If you've lost at love, you know what I'm talking about.

    Who can heal that kind of pain? Only one and His name is Jesus Christ. Ask Him to heal your heart today.

April 17

Answer

Call unto me, and I will answer thee.

Jeremiah 33:3

When you call on the Lord, you are put straight through. You don't have to worry about being put on hold or getting an answering machine. There was a commercial several years ago, where a woman dressed in white was sitting at a desk answering the phone. Some one called who was on fire and she put them straight through to God. It was funny at the time, but sadly, there will be millions of people who will be experiencing fire and it'll be too late for them. A decision needs to be made today while you still have the time.

I saw a saying the other day that said, "When Satan calls. Let God answer." That's a good one.

Who will be answering for you?

April 18

Goodness

He satisfieth the longing soul, and filleth the hungry soul with goodness.

Psalm 107:9

There was a time in my life where things were spinning out-of-control and it was like I was on an out-of-control carousel. I just wanted off. Everyone desires peace. Peace is hard to come by in this world, but it is obtainable. The only source of peace is God.

I learned to hand over my burdens to God because He knows what to do with them. I was burning the candle at both ends and I had to decide to give up my job. The stress was killing me. Not everyone can quit his or her job, so do the next best thing by asking God for help.

What is a hungry soul? It's someone who is seeking God and only God can feed the soul. God will fill the empty spot inside with love, joy, and peace.

Do you have an empty void in your heart?

April 19

Golden Rule

As ye would that men should do to you, do ye also to them.
Luke 6:31

This verse alone has kept me from doing things to others that I thought they deserved. Revenge is a big problem for people. They fill the need to get back at those who have harmed them. They want to even the score. That's human nature. But that doesn't make it right.

I've learned to turn people over to God. After all He is the judge. God will decide what they deserve and He'll punish them. It's not your place to take matters into your own hands. God took care of some matters for me and I couldn't have even come close to what God did. Let God have your burdens.

What will you give Him today?

April 20

Fall

Though he fall he shall not be utterly cast down: for the Lord upholdeth him with His hand.

Psalm 37:24

Sometimes we stumble but it hurts less when God is there to help us up. We have to learn to dust ourselves off and move on.

Seven months after I lost my left eye, I fell in our sunroom and broke my arm and shoulder. You've seen the commercial, "I've fallen and I can't get up!" That was me! Luckily my husband had come home for something and found me lying in the floor crying. He told me to get up so we could go to the hospital and get checked out; but I couldn't get up. If my husband had not helped me up, I would still be there. That was a very painful experience. It's not likely I'll ever forget that fall.

In this verse, it's not talking about a physical fall but a fall from grace. We disappoint God over and over, but He is there for us. He is there to welcome us back into the fold, no matter what we've done. Ask God for forgiveness and then move on. Sometimes we're harder on ourselves, but get over it!

April 21

Peace

For God is not the author of confusion, but of peace.
1 Corinthians 14:33

We know who is the master of confusion and it's not God. Satan just loves to make us miserable! He wants to see you sweat and ring your hands over even the smallest problems. Satan wants to inflict the most pain possible. When we give our lives to Christ, He probably throws a fit. He can't stand for us to accept Jesus Christ as our Savior.

Peace is yours for the asking. What are you waiting for? You can have it now and forever. Don't let Satan steal it!

April 22

Fear

The Lord is my light and my salvation; whom shall I fear? The Lord is the strength of my life; of whom shall I be afraid?
Psalm 27:1

When God is on your side then you shouldn't fear anything or anyone. What do you fear? Give it to God and let Him deal with it.

Fear is something that we all know. Some people live in fear because of something that happened to them and they can't cope with it. If this is the case, there are good psychologists that can help. God wants us to use the doctors that have been made available for us. I would choose a Christian therapist. Seek God's guidance and He will not steer you in the wrong direction. God loves you and wants you healed and whole.

April 23

Pray

Pray to thy Father which is in secret; and the Father which seeth in secret shall reward thee openly.

Matthew 6:6

I'm learning to pray more in secret. Everybody doesn't need to know all the details. Sometimes in Sunday school we say we have an unspoken request and that's all that's needed. God knows what the request is without saying it out loud. God will still know your request. No where does it say that a prayer has to be verbalized. God knows our thoughts and every need.

I've been praying in secret for some time now and God is finally answering my request. It's awesome when God answers us. He probably got tired of me asking for this one request, but I know it was also the desire of God's heart. Don't give up.

April 24

Sinners

God commendeth His love toward us, in that, while we were yet sinners, Christ died for us.

Romans 5:8

God has always loved us. We haven't done anything to deserve it. It is called grace and it's free. He loved us so much that He sent His only Son here to save the world. It's mind-blowing. Love that great only comes from above! More than likely you'll never see it here on earth between humans. God's love is supernatural. It's out-of-this-world! Do you know just how much He really loves you?

April 25

Confess

If we confess our sins, He is faithful and just to forgive us our sins, and to cleanse us from all unrighteousness.

1 John 1:9

Does God pick and choose which sins He wants to forgive, or does He forgive them all? The Bible says He will forgive all your sins. Make sure you are really remorseful or it doesn't work. Remember God knows if you're sorry or not.

God can erase anything you've done. I was thrilled to learn that they are erased forever, never to be remembered again. It would be nice if we could erase our sins from our memories, but we can't for some reason. Maybe we want to punish ourselves for being so stupid. If God can forget, we should try to forget, also.

April 26

First

Many that are first, shall be last; and the last shall be first.
Matthew 19:30

This verse should make everyone happy that has found themselves dead last or the least. We'll be perfect in heaven in every way and we'll never have to worry what position we're in ever again. We'll all be equal in heaven. What a glorious day that will be!

I was born last of five and I was treated like I was the least by my siblings. I didn't receive the awards they won and I didn't have the grades they had, but none have written a book and this is my third adult book with ten children's books waiting to be illustrated. I wouldn't trade myself with any of them. I am very happy with the way God made me. God doesn't make junk! What about you?

April 27

Confess

If thou shalt confess with thy mouth the Lord Jesus, and shalt believe in thine heart that God hath raised Him from the dead, thou shalt be saved.

Romans 10:9

Your eternity depends on whom you know and what you believe. Do you believe Jesus is the Son of God? Do you believe Jesus is at the right hand of God, the Father?

Lee Strobel was an atheist until he set out to prove that Jesus was not God's Son. In the process, Lee became a believer. Lee couldn't find any evidence that Jesus was a regular man. People find it very hard to believe in the virgin birth. Many think a Roman soldier fathered Jesus, while others think Joseph was his real father. People also think that the disciples stole Jesus' body after the crucifixion. I can only imagine the rumors that were spread during that moment of time. Some believed at the moment of crucifixion because of the absence of the sun, the earthquake, and the tearing of the curtain in the temple. Oh, how they must have felt when they realized they had killed a Savior that had come to save them!

April 28

Restoreth

He leadeth me beside the still waters. He restoreth my soul.

Psalm 23:2-3

Does your soul need restoring? I know who can restore your soul like it was new. I've had mine restored many times and boy, does it feel great! It's so awesome to have a Savior who has such wonderful powers. There is nothing He can't do. He's just waiting for you to ask. You don't need a new outfit to feel good. You need a soul makeover.

If you would like examples of His work, there are many in the Bible.

April 29

Look Up!

I will lift up mine eyes unto the hills, from whence cometh my help.
Psalm 121:1

I know where my help lives. My helper lives in heaven. He's waiting to come get us. Only God knows the date, but someday He'll call Jesus to His side and say, "It's time to bring them home." Jesus will rush right out to meet us in the sky and I can't wait! I'm ready right this very moment to meet my Maker face to face. We are going to have a huge feast in heaven, like none you have ever witnessed. No need to worry if you'll gain weight, either. You won't have to worry, if we'll run out of food, either. Remember everything will be perfect right down to the conversation. The guest of honor, is someone you already know. It'll be our Father, Jesus Christ.

April 30

Safety

The beloved of the Lord shall dwell in safely by Him.
Deuteronomy 33:12

Where does it say we'll dwell? It doesn't say, we'll dwell behind Him but beside Him. Jesus is beside me every day and takes every step I take. He doesn't tell us to run ahead and He'll show up later. He wants to be as close as He can get to us.

Today security has become a hot topic with terrorist breathing down our necks. We don't know from one minute to the next when they will strike. I refuse to, live in fear like they want. I know I'm not leaving here till it's my time. I know whom watches over me at all time. I do believe the Lord is coming soon. It's not soon enough for me. See you at the gate!

May 1

Word

The grass whithereth, and the flower thereof falleth away: But the word of the Lord endureth for ever.

1 Peter 1:24-25

Any body who has worked in a garden knows how quickly a flower or plant can die. They just don't last long. I worked in an acre garden until I went off to college. My father was a soil conservationist and he loved growing vegetables.

Now that food prices are going up due to the high gas prices, more and more people are talking about starting gardens. I have no intentions of ever working in a garden again because my back won't allow it. I'll just buy some veggies from my friends.

All plants have their designed time to produce and then die. God is using this illustration to impress upon us that plants may die, but His word will never die. God's word has applied to people from the beginning of time and will until the earth will be destroyed. Everything you need to know is in the Bible.

May 2

One Sinner

There is joy in the presence of the angels of God over one sinner that repenteth.

Luke 15:10

Some day we'll get to see what happens behind the scenes. I can only imagine right now what the angels do when someone repents of their sins. We don't really know joy because reality starts to set in and ruins the mood. In heaven there won't be anything to ruin the moment.

Take your happiest moment and multiple it. Here's a good activity for you to do. You'll need a journal, a pen, and some quiet time. Write at the top of the page: Things that make me happy. Start writing down all the things you can think of. Before you're through, you'll be in a better mood. Any time you start feeling blue, get out your journal. It really works. You might want to pass this activity on to a friend or family member who has trouble with depression. They'll love you for it!

May 3

Watch

Watch therefore: for ye know not what hour your Lord doth come.
Matthew 24:42

Whenever I have the time, I like to look at the sky. As a child, I use to make things out of the clouds, especially on long trips to go see my grandparents on the gulf coast. It helped me pass the time. I taught my girls to watch clouds, also.

I have a picture of Jesus in the clouds and I love to stare at it. I added the words, Jesus is coming soon to the bottom of the picture and put it on my bulletin board, where I have pictures of loved ones who have gone on ahead of me. When I look at the board, I'm reminded of the wonderful memories. I also have pictures of my beloved pets at the bottom.

We have no idea when our time will be up unless a doctor has given us an estimated time because of a terminal illness. Even then it's an educated guess.

Unfortunately, some people think they'll wait till they are old before they decide to turn their life over to Christ. I would like to know what measure they will use to determine when it's the appropriate time. What about accidents? Once that last breath is taken, there's no turning back unless you are Don Piper. Don didn't know he had died till he got to the gate. There wasn't time to ask God to save him. Thank goodness he was already a Christian.

May 4

Forgiven

Be ye kind one to another, tenderhearted, forgiving one another, even as God for Christ's sake hath forgiven you.

Ephesians 4:32

Forgiveness is like a four letter word to some people. It's probably one of the hardest things that God requires of us. I know I struggled with it for years. I knew what God wanted me to do, but it's easier said than done. I had an easier time stopping my smoking and drinking than forgiveness. Unforgiveness will make you physically sick. It's like poison to your body. As long as you have unforgiveness, the person who harmed you wins. They could even be dead and they are reaching out to you from the grave. Put a stop to it right now. Ask God to help you forgive them. Then and only then will God forgive you. He will help you with this matter, because He wants it so badly for you. He wants you happy and healthy.

Who do you need to forgive today?

May 5

Sacrifice

Hereby perceive we the love of God, because He laid down His life for us.

1 John 3:16

I've guessed you've noticed all the love messages so far that God made sure made it into the Bible. He wants you to know without a doubt just how much He loves you. If God can send His only Son to die for you, then what can you do for Him and His Son? Without this amazing act of love, there would be no chance of us being made righteous enough to get into heaven. You can't earn a pass. You can't buy a pass, either.

There's no list in the Bible of things you have to do to get into heaven. If works were required, there would be a list. There are religions out there that think you can earn a place equal to God. They will be sadly disappointed when they get to the other side.

Spend some time today deciding what you can do for Christ. It's really not hard.

May 6

Rest

Come unto me, all ye that labour and are heavy laden, and I will give you rest.

Matthew 11:28

    You could stop anyone on the street and ask them what they need and I bet it wouldn't take long for someone to say they need rest or sleep. The world is moving at a very fast pace. Compared to the Bible days, it seems like we're spinning out of control. One place it shows up is on the road. People are getting more aggressive each day! We didn't know what road rage was when I was growing up. It's gotten bad in Memphis, TN. It's gotten too dangerous for me to drive with just one eye. I have trouble even here in a small town.

    Are you heavy laden from your work or from family matters? Everybody has problems. The only one willing to take them from you is God. Try it. If you don't like the freedom, take your problems back. It's worth a try.

May 7

Wait

Wait on the Lord, and keep His way, and He shall exalt thee.
Psalm 37:34

Patience was never a virtue for me, but over time God has showed me how important it is to wait on Him. God's timing is perfect. We make a lot of mistakes by jumping head first into something, when it would have been better to wait on God.

I don't know why we attempt to do God's work for Him. We should just turn the situation over to Him and remove ourselves from the mix. God created the world in six days and rested on the seventh. Did He need your help in creating this world? I've got news for you. He doesn't need your help now, either. He can handle all your problems!

May 8

Peace

Let the peace of God rule in your hearts.

Colossians 3:15

This is one lesson I should have learned early in my life. I lived in so much chaos with seven people in a very small house with one bathroom. Even eating was stressful. If you didn't get what you wanted on the first go round, you didn't see it again. I developed a nervous stomach from all the stress.

It wasn't until I sought professional help for the stomach and colon, that the stress was managed. Even today, I have to take nexium before I eat. Look at all the prescriptions we as Americans take daily. We're probably the most medicated people on this planet. What we pay for meds is highway robbery.

God wants a peaceful life for us. We have to want it, for it to happen. I've made up my mind that I will live in peace for the rest of my life no matter what happens. How bad do you want peace in your life?

May 9

Unto Me

In as much as ye have done it unto one of the least of these my brethren, ye have done it unto me.

Matthew 25:40

How many times have we hurt people? How many times have we looked the other way when passing a homeless person on the street? How many times have we refused to invite someone into our house? How many times have we lied to others? How many times have we refused to give our money or time to a worthwhile project? I'm sure there have been countless times when we have been guilty of all of the above.

The only way to break yourself from these bad habits is to put Jesus' face on each person you come in contact with or ask God to change your heart. Remember character is whom you are when no one is looking. Develop good character that you can live with.

May 10

Good Heart

Love one another with a pure heart fervently.

1 Peter 1:22

A pure heart is not easily achieved. Can a person with a bad heart ever have a chance at developing a pure heart? Only with the help of God. All things are possible with Christ.

Every day we need to work toward being more like Christ and a good place to start is the heart. I believe the heart is more important than your IQ. You can learn all kinds of facts and information to raise your IQ, but it will take hard work to develop a pure heart. God doesn't just wave a magic wand and instantly change your heart. You have to work with God and for God. You have to die to self.

May 11

Sorrow

Ye now therefore have sorrow: but I will see you again, and your heart shall rejoice, and your joy no man taketh from you.
John 16:22

    Here's a wonderful promise that God has made for you, even though you may be suffering or grieving; God promises to return to you your joy and happiness. Joy that he says can't be taken away from you. I'm there now.
    I use to let people control my emotions. I wanted to please everyone, which is not humanly possible. People were very mean to me and said things that weren't true. They have slandered me in a very mean way. Do they realize what they have done? No. No clue, whatsoever! No apologies, either. I've turned them over to God so He can deal with them and their sin against me. I now have unspeakable joy and happiness and they can't take that away from me, because God gave it to me. I have lived this verse, so please believe every word of it! God's word is nothing but the truth!

May 12

Worship

God is a spirit, and they that worship Him must worship Him in spirit and in truth.

John 4:24

God doesn't do things half way so don't think you're going to get away with only half a commitment. God wants all of you. You can't hide anything from Him.

If you're going to work with God, you will have to speak the truth in all manners. No little white lies or half- truths.

I know people who attend church for looks. They don't want the community to know they are not sincere in their beliefs. So they walk through the motions and pretend to be worshipping. They are wasting their time, but maybe while they are in church, they will feel God wooing them. What better place for a non-believer to be than surrounded by Christians.

Remember in <u>Left Behind</u> the associate preacher was left behind? He had not fully given his life to Christ. He knew the scriptures frontward and backwards. He knew there was a God, but he had not accepted Jesus Christ as his Lord and Savior. I loved the CD message that T. D. Jakes had left for those left behind. Some people believe people will be given a second chance, but I've heard others say if they miss the rapture; that's it. I wouldn't want to be left behind and find out I was doomed to hell. Whom do you serve today?

May 13

Perfected

If we love one another, God dwelleth in us, and His love is perfected in us.

1 John 4:12

If you hate someone, that's not a good sign for a Christian. My mother wouldn't allow us to say we hated anyone. She said you can dislike his or her ways, but it's a sin to hate anyone.

God can not live where there is hate in the heart. I've witnessed people who had so much hate for people, it was horrible to be in their presence.

Instead of fussing and complaining about everything, try finding the good in everything and see what a difference it makes in your day. God says that a cheerful heart is like medicine. Some experts have suggested putting a rubber band on your wrist and when you complain; put the band on the other wrist. Try to get through a day without having to change the rubber band. It's not as easy as you think. I don't consider myself a negative person and I had trouble with this exercise.

God wants you to be a happy person and let people see Him shine through you. Start right now. Give me a "huge" smile! Now give five people in your day a smile.

May 14

Darkness

God who commanded the light to shine out of darkness, hath shined in our hearts, to give the light of the knowledge of the glory of God.
2 Corinthians 4:6

Darkness was all that was here before God created the earth and the heavens. Imagine yourself standing by God when He spoke and things suddenly appeared. What power!

I hope there's a huge screen in heaven and we can hit rewind and see creation. Wouldn't that be awesome?

God says the same light that filled the universe, fills our hearts. How is your light? Can anyone see God's light in you? Maybe you need to turn up the light for all to see.

While our mission team was in Ghana recently, a man told the team that the people there were seeing God through their love and actions. The people of Ghana knew our team left the comforts of our air-conditioning and traveled halfway around the world just to come help them build some churches. That is agape love! God is love!

May 15

Light

The Lord shall be unto thee an everlasting light, and thy God thy glory.

Isaiah 60:19

We deal with light on a daily basis, but it's not the everlasting kind. I can't stand it when our electricity goes out and unfortunately it happens a lot more than I like. Just recently a storm blew through and I sat in the dark for five hours. I kept telling my husband, I want a generator.

I was scared of the dark when I was a child. I don't know what happened to cause me to be afraid, but it use to terrify me. I would refuse to walk into a dark room. As an adult, I don't like to come home to a dark house so I leave on some lights.

The term everlasting light means our Lord will not fade away. He is always there. All the pictures I've seen of Jesus have a glow radiating from all sides. I saw a church sign that said, "The Son is always shining."

How is the light where you are?

May 16

Strength

The Lord is my strength and song, and He is become my salvation.
Exodus 15:2

    I can do nothing apart from my Lord. I was born with a tumor behind my eye and when I hit puberty, it started growing. I can remember at 13, I started losing my balance. No one thought to check me for a tumor. How I ever hit a basket in basketball was a miracle. In track, I even had trouble staying in my lane when I ran. My family just thought I was clumsy, because I tripped a lot. I even ran into door facings. It wasn't until I was in New York City on July 4, 2000, that I knew something was terribly wrong. After arriving home, I went to Semmes Murphy for tests.

    My doctor sent me immediately to Methodist South Hospital in Southaven, MS. Once I returned the next day with x-rays in hand, did the doctor realize that I had a very rare tumor behind my left eye.

    How did I get to this point with a tumor growing behind my eye? Only by the grace of God, go I. God gave me the strength to play sports, drive, and take care of myself and my family. Even when I couldn't return to work, God opened another door for me. This is my third adult book. God knew my weakness was English, but that didn't matter to Him. God can use anyone as long as they have a willing heart. God will supply the strength.

May 17

Kindness

Blessed be the Lord: for He hath showed me His marvelous kindness.
Psalm 31:21

Kindness goes a long way in today's world. It's easy to get caught up in all the business and stress of life. I've noticed in the reality shows, they are pitting players against each other. We don't need to encourage people to be mean to others. It's better to show kindness to everyone we meet.

Jesus has been nothing but kind to us and we should follow His lead. Jesus always spoke in a kind gentle voice. They say you can get more bees with honey.

I told a lady that stocks the dog food section at Walmart today that I had been thinking about her and her sick son. She said that was a first for her. I thought, surely not. How hard is it to say a kind word to someone who needs it? A kind word said to someone who is thinking about suicide can make a difference in a life.

Say something kind to several people today and see what happens.

May 18

Treasure

Where your treasure is, there will your heart be also.
Matthew 6:21

If you want to find out what your treasure is, look in your checkbook and see where most of your money goes. Some people live through their children, some buy expensive toys, some collect rare items, some travel all over the world, while others look like they stepped out of Vogue. Owning nice things is not a sin, but the love of money is the root of evil.

It's better to store up your treasures in heaven where they will not rust or ruin. What is your treasure?

May 19

Water

Whosoever drinketh of the water that I shall give him shall never thirst; but the water that I give him shall be in him a well of water springing up into everlasting life.

John 4:14

What Jesus is telling us is that if we follow Him, He will take care of us and we shall not want for anything. He will provide for us and take care of our every need, not just for a season; but forever. Jesus is not just a flash in the pan Savior, but He is here for today and tomorrow. Jesus is forever.

My only regret is that my faith wasn't stronger when I was faced with major problems as a child and a teenager. I didn't handle things as well as I would have liked. I can't go back so I chalk it up to life's lessons.

Now, I live for Christ Jesus. Better late than never. Some will never come to Christ and they'll never know the joy and happiness that could have been theirs.

May 20

Dwell

I will dwell in the midst of thee, saith the Lord.
Zechariah 2:10

If you could have one wish, what would it be? Having Jesus with me all the time everywhere I go is at the top of my list. He is the most powerful man that has ever existed. He's more powerful than a genie in a bottle. A genie grants three wishes, but Jesus grants us our desires with an endless supply of dreams. Nothing compares to Jesus.

I'm so looking forward to being in His presence. I haven't lived a perfect life and when my time is over; I'll enter into a perfect place called heaven. Won't you come with me?

May 21

Brotherly Love

Let brotherly love continue.

Hebrews 13:1

Surround yourself with brothers and sisters in Christ and you can get a head start on heaven. People think it is boring being a Christian, but that's a lie straight from Satan. My brothers and sisters in Christ have a blast.

Have you heard about Emmaus? It's a retreat about Jesus and it's nothing like any other retreat you've ever attended. You will have so much fun, you won't want to go home when it's over. The great part about this retreat is there's something for you at all the future walks, so it never ends. I've been working Emmaus Walks for twelve years and it has changed my life. I was racked with depression for years because of childhood abuse. At Emmaus, I laid all my burdens at the foot of the cross. I've met brothers and sisters in Christ that I would have never met till I got to heaven. Check with your church and see if they sponsor the Emmaus Walks. All fifty states have them. Remember that it's all about Jesus, not you.

May 22

Justified

Being justified by faith, we have peace with God through our Lord Jesus Christ.

Romans 5:1

Here's another lesson on peace. Can you ever get tired of talking about peace? Peace is something we all desire, but so few have. Unbelievers don't know peace. Peace comes from surrendering your life to Christ and allowing Him to take control. While Jesus was here, he experienced all the emotions we have and faced problems just like ours. Jesus wasn't born with a silver spoon in His mouth. He was born to a lowly carpenter in a lowly manger with His parents on the run. Why was He born in such a lowly manner? There's a reason for everything. Jesus was born for all people, no matter their social status or anything else. If Jesus had been born to a wealthy family then those lower than Him would not have related to Him. They would have felt that Jesus was out of touch with them and had no compassion for their plight.

Peace only comes from above. How can Christians enjoy peace when the world is at war with each other? His name is Jesus. If you don't have peace, the missing piece is Jesus.

May 23

Safety

When thou passest through the waters, I will be with thee; and through the rivers, they shall not overflow thee.

Isaiah 43:2

The people of the midwest really need this verse, because they are experiencing floods that have broken a hundred year record. I've seen a lot of floods, but this is really bad. People are losing everything they own. If you've never lost everything, it's hard to understand the devastation that occurs; especially if you don't have insurance or your insurance doesn't cover rising water. Katrina victims know this kind of loss and some are still battling their insurance companies.

Job is a perfect example of how to survive a major loss. Job lost all his property, livestock, servants, and children. The only thing that God spared was his wife. People thought Job had done something terribly wrong to deserve such wrath, but it was Satan that asked permission to have his way with Job. Satan wanted to prove that Job really didn't love God with his whole heart and thought he could turn Job against God. God knew Job's heart. That's why God allowed this test. We will all have trials and tribulations. If you love God with your whole heart, you will pass with flying colors. God will restore what you've lost. God always provides for His children.

May 24

Helper

The Lord is my helper, and I will not fear what man shall do unto me.
Hebrews 13:6

Unfortunately, there will always be someone who will harm you or wish you harm. People become jealous. Christians should not fit in this area, but I've known some that from time to time participate in these activities. Christians are suppose to encourage, lift up, and support those who are in need. Our example was Jesus. He loved everyone. He was kind, compassionate, loving, caring, and supportive.

People will make mistakes. They will call you names and do things they will have to ask God for forgiveness; but that's not your problem. God is the judge and that's His department. Turn the abusers over to the judge. Don't live in fear of what others will do to you. Walk in faith that God will take care of all your problems today, tomorrow, and in the future. God doesn't need your help. He just needs a willing heart to release to Him your problems. He'll take it from there. Satan is the only one who wants you to live in fear. Tell him where he can go!

May 25

Prepare

If I go and prepare a place for you, I will come again, and receive you unto myself; that where I am there ye may be also.

John 14:3

I love this verse. The disciples were so heart sick and broken when Christ was placed on the cross; but they didn't fully understand what Jesus had been trying to tell them. Jesus tried to prepare them for what was to come. They had no clue.

When Jesus returned from the grave, they were in awe. They thought He would remain with them, but soon found out that He couldn't stay. They wanted to go with Him. Jesus explained why they couldn't go. They had a job to do first.

Jesus is preparing a place for us and I can't wait to see it. He has promised to come again and He can't lie. Someday, He will come for us and we'll never be separated ever again. We'll live in eternity forever and ever. Amen!

Don't sit on the couch waiting for Him. There's work to be done until it's your time to go. Keep busy. His kingdom depends on it. Jesus is counting on you.

May 26

Abundance

A man's life consisteth not in the abundance of the things which be possesseth.

Luke 12:15

    What we own or any honors that we have won do not determine our status with Christ. God sees us as equal children. God is an equal opportunity God.

    Remember the last shall be first. God doesn't care how much money you have in the bank or whether you wear designer clothes, or wear diamonds. It's not what's on the outside that matters. It's what's on the inside that matters to God. Do you love God? Do you love His Son? Are you willing to follow Jesus Christ? Are you willing to keep God's commandments? Are you willing to die to self?

    You are the only one who can answer these questions. Decide today, whom you will serve.

May 27

Thanks

In everything give thanks: for this is the will of God in Christ Jesus concerning you.

1 Thessalonians 5:18

This is a tall order for most people. Giving thanks for sickness or loss of all your possessions is extremely hard for anyone. At the moment, you might not feel thankful; but over time you might look back over the situation and see some positive things that developed from your loss. It takes a very strong Christian to reach this point in your faith. It is attainable. Remember all things are possible with Christ.

As we mature as Christians, we are constantly thriving to do God's will, not ours. This verse says, it's God will to give thanks for everything. Next time you're faced with difficulty; try giving thanks and see what happens.

When a loved one dies, we are not to be thankful that they died; but we can be thankful for the time that we shared. I only had sixteen years to enjoy my mother, but I'll live with her for eternity. I'm thankful my mother was a beautiful Christian and that she raised me in the church. She made sure I got the foundation I would need in life. I am so thankful! I am blessed beyond measure.

May 28

Possible

With God all things are possible.

Matthew 19:26

How many times do we say, "No, way?" Yes, way! All things are possible through Christ. There is nothing He can't do. He created the world, so why would you think He couldn't handle your problems? He can do it all! He can move mountains, part seas, bring people back from the grave, and heal people who are dying. If you don't believe He is that powerful, then ask yourself what is blocking your belief. The problem lies with you not Him. Spend some time in reflection and see if you can uncover the real problem. You hold the answer.

May 29

Live

For to me to live is Christ, and to die is gain.
                                          Philippians 1:21

You've heard me say several times, "You have to die to self." In order to serve Christ, He needs to be the controller of your heart. If you are operating in your own best interest, then Christ is not the center of your life. Christ needs to lead.

When you hear, "Let God be your pilot", it means the same thing. Let God have the controls. God sees things we don't see. God understands things we don't understand. God knows what's best. Put your thoughts and feelings aside and let God's power take over. You will probably find yourself outside your comfort zone, but if that's where God needs you to go; then go. God will make us fishers of men and sometimes that means getting out of the boat. The fish are in the deeper water, not the shallow. Go wherever He leads.

May 30

Troubled

Peace I leave with you, my peace I give unto you: not as the world giveth, give I unto you. Let not your heart be troubled, neither let it be afraid.

John 14:27

Here we go again. Peace is a valuable commodity in this world. As time goes on, it will be harder and harder to find. You will need to hold on to it with all your might. Satan will try to steal it from you. Satan loves misery and misery loves company.

Satan had it made in heaven but his desire to take God's place ruined everything for him and his followers. He has spent all this time roaming the earth causing misery for billions of people. When you feel an evil presence, you have the power through the Holy Spirit to make Satan flee in all directions. I use a Bible verse or song with Jesus' name because Satan can't stand the name of Jesus.

Don't let the problems of this world weigh you down. We're just passing through. This is not our permanent home.

Don't let anything cause you to fear. When I was first married, I didn't like being out of sight from my husband. I had already lost my mother and I was losing my grandparents left and right. I had a fear of abandonment. God has helped me over the years to understand that I'll never be alone, as long as I have Him in my heart. Yes, people live and they die, but if they are Christians, we'll only be separated for a while.

May 31

Created

Thou art worthy, O Lord, to receive glory and honour and power; for thou hast created all things, and for thy pleasure they are and were created.
Revelation 4:11

How does it feel to know we were created for God's pleasure? I think it's awesome! We are made worthy to be called His, because Christ died for our sins. He loves us, no matter what we've done in the past. He erases our mistakes to remember them no more. Amen! Thank goodness, he does not keep records on forgiven sins.

What about your attitude? Is it an attitude that God would want to be around? Are you happy or sad? God loves a cheerful heart. He didn't create you so He could stick pins and needles in you. He loves you! He created you out of love. How do you repay Him?

June 1

Love

Thou shalt love they neighbor as thyself.

Matthew 22:39

    We recently studied this lesson at church and talk about hitting me between the eyes. It's hard to love a neighbor when they don't respect your property and lets their dog dig holes in your yard and leaves waste on your sidewalk. I've tried to be nice, but it's not working. I've asked God to give me the strength to be the Christian neighbor I need to be.

    Why do you think God requires us to be good neighbors? If we can't be kind to our neighbors, then how are we going to be kind to anyone else that crosses our path? We are to show love to everyone so they'll know we are Christians.

June 2

Free

Ye shall know the truth, and the truth shall make you free.
John 8:32

  The truth is that Jesus is the Son of God and that He came to save the world. By believing in Christ, you are set free from the bondage of Satan. With the power of the Holy Spirit within you, the chains of Satan can not work on you. You have to be a willing partner with Satan to sin. Satan can't force you to sin. It's your choice.
  Choose this day, which you will serve. You can't serve both. Christ can not live in your heart where there is evil. Christ demands to be the only occupant. Choose Christ and you'll be free.

June 3

Gift

For by grace are ye saved through faith; and that not of yourselves: it is the gift of God.

Ephesians 2:8

Gifts are free. You don't pay to be saved. You don't earn or work for your salvation. It's totally free. It's up to every person to freely accept the gift of salvation from God.

There have been many arguments over this subject, but this verse says it all. We are saved by grace and not any acts on our own accord. We simply believe and accept Christ. Then we confess our sins and ask God for forgiveness. It's so simple but so hard for some people to do. They will pay a very dear price for not accepting God's Son. The way of the world is death. Death is separation from God. If people knew what hell is like, they would not spend another moment separated from God. The sad thing is they will find out too late. Where are you going? Smoking or non-smoking?

June 4

Deed

Let us not love in word, neither in tongue; but in deed and in truth.
1 John 3:18

So many people speak words that are not a true reflection of their feelings. People say day after day that they love you, when really they love only themselves. God warns us not to do that.

God wants us to truly love one another and show it through our actions and speak it in truth. You can't fool God. You might be able to fool those around you, but not God. He knows every thought or word that you have spoken. God holds you accountable for everything you do.

My daughter once questioned me when I stopped to give a couple, holding a sign on the side of the road, money. She said they were probably ripping everybody off. I told her that I was giving in faith that they really needed money to buy food, like their sign said. If they were dishonest, then God would deal with them, not me. We are instructed to help the poor, needy, and widows. God will take care of those who are dishonest.

June 5

Rejoice

Rejoice, and be exceedingly glad: for great is your reward in heaven.
Matthew 5:12

    I'm learning more and more each day how to be exceedingly glad. It's not easy in this world. This world is full of heartache and sadness. God says that if we'll rejoice anyway, he'll reward us in heaven. I don't know about you, but I think the rewards will be special, just because they are from God. God doesn't make junk. So as hard as it may be, I'm going to rejoice and be glad in everything I do. I had my joy stolen from me as a child and I'm not willing to let anyone or anything steal it again. Teach yourself how to be happy every day.

June 6

The Truth

I am the way, the truth, and the life.

John 14:6

These were the words of Jesus. He is telling the world that He is the only way to the Father. The world would like for you to believe otherwise, but the way of the world is death. To believe in Christ is life and we shall live forever with Him in paradise. This is the truth.

I was just watching "The Nativity Story" and thinking how simple life seemed in the Bible days. Sure they had some of the same problems we have today, but it was an honorable life. Today there are so many distractions and temptations that hinder us. That's why it's so important to make quiet times for us to draw near to our Lord and Savior. He longs to spend time with us. I know time is valuable, but time with our Lord is more valuable than anything you have or desire to own. He longs to be in your presence. He longs to hear from you. He adores you! This is the truth.

June 7

Love

Neither death, nor life,...nor height, nor depth, nor any other creature, shall be able to separate us from the love of God.
Romans 8:38-39

Jesus was born the foundation of life for all humanity. Nothing can change that. No creature, no war, no death, can keep us from God. Nothing is more powerful than our Father. That alone should be reason enough for you to sleep well at night.

God is on the throne and all is well with my soul. I know and understand the truth and that's all that matters. No one can take my God away from me. Robbers may come and take away everything I own, but they can't take away my God or my faith. I pray the same for you. A person, who realizes the love God has for them, has everything they need. What more could you ask for, except come quickly, Lord?

June 8

Midst

Where two or three are gathered together in my name, there am I in the midst of them.

Matthew 18:20

Remember the next time you are praying with someone, that Jesus is there, also. Learn to feel His presence. Seek Him and He shall make Himself known to you.

I prayed while I was waiting to have my first heart catheterization. My doctor was running forty minutes late and I was freezing to death. I was shaking so bad my teeth were chattering. I looked at the clock and knew people were praying for me at that moment. I asked God to allow me to feel the prayers that were being said for me. Instantly, a red, hot feeling passed from the top of my head all the way down to my feet. I knew it was a gift from God. As I was soaking up the moment, my tech noticed I wasn't shaking anymore. He quietly entered the room and leaned over me. He said, "Mrs. Gaines are you still with us?" I opened my eye and said, "Yes." The tech wanted to know what just happened. He knew something powerful happened right before his eyes. I explained to him my prayer and how God answered it. I wasn't the only one in that room blessed by the hand of God that day.

Seek His face.

June 9

Fear Not

Trust in the Lord with all thine heart; and lean not unto thine own understanding. In all thy ways acknowledge Him, and He shall direct thy paths.

Proverbs 3:5-6

We will never know the answer to all our questions or understand why certain things happen to us, but God knows all. We have to trust Him in all things. He does not wish to harm us. He does allow things to happen for a reason. We may have to wait till we get to heaven to understand why. Does it really matter, why?

I cried out why to God, when my mother died at age 50. Why doesn't change what happened. I had to learn to trust God that it was her time to go. She had lived a full life. She touched countless lives in the 20 years that she taught school. People still talk about her and her kindness. She made her time here count. What are you doing with your time?

June 10

Overcome

In the world ye shall have tribulation: but be of good cheer; I have overcome the world.

John 16:33

    I don't know about you, but I'm ecstatic over the fact that Christ took back control when He died on the cross. Satan didn't want Christ to be our sacrifice. Satan tried to get Christ to stay by offering Him all the land that He could see from the mountaintop. Christ knew His mission. That's why He stayed on the cross. He had the power to come down. Christ knew why He was here and carried the divine plan through to completion. He suffered for you and me. He loved us enough to give up His life for us. Has anyone ever died just for you? I doubt it.

    What can you do today for Christ, who died for you?

June 11

Peace

To be spiritually minded is life and peace.

Romans 8:6

    Spiritually minded in a corrupt world is not easy. The Bible never says life will be easy for the Christians. The Holy Spirit comes to live in the hearts of Christians, which gives us the power from within to resist temptations. The Holy Spirit brings eternal life and peace. You shall never thirst with the living water dwelling within you. He will provide whatever you need.
    What do you need today?

June 12

Fishers

Follow me, and I will make you fishers of men.
Matthew 4:19

Even if you think you can't bring anyone to Christ, He will give you the words to say. Follow His lead. All you have to do is be a willing servant. God will provide everything you need to go in His name. Let the love of Christ shine for others to see and tell others what He has done for you. Let them hear the joy in your voice and let them feel the love in your heart. If they reject Christ as their Savior, it'll be their fault, not yours. Speak the truth. It's up to each person to accept or deny Christ. Every time a soul is saved, there is a huge celebration in heaven. One day we'll rejoice with Christ, our loved ones, brothers, and sisters in Christ, and the angels. One day will come when no one else can be saved. Until then keep telling others about Christ. Our work will not be done until He comes for us. Use the time you have left wisely.

June 13

One Master

Thou shalt worship the Lord thy God and Him only shalt thou serve.
Matthew 4:10

God makes it very clear in the Bible that He is the only God and the only one that we are to serve. The world serves around 3,000 different Gods. I would like to know how some of these Gods were created. Somebody has a creative mind. People believe what suits them best. You can't pick and choose what verses you want to believe. The Bible is the word of God and if you change any part of it to fit your lifestyle or what you want to believe; it says you will suffer the worst death. You don't mess with God. The Bible was written to help us understand God and His laws. It wasn't written to entertain us. It was written for instruction. A Bible that is falling apart is usually owned by someone who isn't.

June 14

Thy Way

Teach me thy ways, O Lord; I will walk in thy truth.

Psalm 86:11

Do you have a teachable heart? If not, you need to find out why. You need a teachable heart to follow God. He needs someone who can put themselves aside and work for Him. If you work for the Lord, the retirement plan is out-of-this-world!

The Bible warns us of false prophets in the end times. I've seen some giving themselves credit for healing, when healing comes from the anointed one. I heard a famous preacher say that he gets his anointing from his dead grandparents. He said when he gets low on anointing, he goes to their graves and lays across it. Who does he think he's fooling?

All glory belongs to God. We are nothing apart from God. The apostles were ordinary men designed for greatness. They gave up everything to go and tell the "good news". They were passionate and on fire for the Lord. They were given a gift of speaking in tongue, so they could go out into the world. They healed the sick and raised the dead.

Will you go for Christ?

June 15

Lead

I will lead them in paths that they have not known: I will make darkness light before them, and crooked things straight.

Isaiah 42:16

If you are willing to get out of you comfort zone God will take care of you. My husband hates to fly long distances and it took him 24 hours to travel to Ghana, Africa for a mission trip. While there they spent most of the time in a hotel where there was no air conditioning. Africa has a lot of snakes and I prayed really hard that he would not see one. He hates snakes! Thank goodness, he only saw lizards. He was exhausted when he got home because it took 40 hours of travel to get back. Because he was willing to go for Christ's sake, he had an incredible time in Africa. It was a life-changing trip. He came home with some gorgeous pictures. I wasn't able to make the trip but I felt like I was there in spirit. I covered the team in prayer.

I provided the first donation for the team to build a church in memory of my parents, Raymond and Clara Powell Simpson. I gave my husband a sharpie pen to write their name on a part of the church. My mother made sure I got my foundation right in Christ, so I had their names written on the foundation of the church. Souls will be saved in that church.

What can you do for Christ today?

June 16

Trust

Thou wilt keep him in perfect peace, whose mind is stayed on thee: because he trusted in thee.

Isaiah 26:3

This verse I know because I have put all my trust and faith in God and He has given me perfect peace. I couldn't have created a more perfect peace than what God has done for me. He is willing to do the same for you.

Whatever is blocking your peace, God can remove it. Whatever joy has been stolen, God can return it to you in abundance. There is nothing He can't do. Keep your focus on Jesus. He's the man!

June 17

Kingdom

Behold, the kingdom of God is within you.

Luke 17:21

    Because of this verse, we are instructed to keep the temple holy. God lives within us, so be careful how you treat your body. We do things to our body that we would never dream of doing to our church. Keep your heart clean and keep your mind sober. Eat healthy foods and don't over eat. Exercise is also important. If you are a couch potato, how can you work for Christ? The lost aren't going to show up at your door. A few might but not many.

    What can you do today to improve your temple?

June 18

Clean Heart

Create in me a clean heart, O God; and renew a right spirit within me.
Psalm 51:10

This verse is every Christians' request. If you don't have a clean heart, you can't be a good witness for Christ. People will see the evil within you and won't desire to become a Christian. We are to be more like Christ as each day passes.

It's easy to have a bad spirit, but hard to have a right spirit. We need God to create the right spirit within us. God is a spirit. He is the right spirit to choose. You can never go wrong with God.

June 19

New Creature

If any man be in Christ, he is a new creature: old things are passed away; all things are become new.
2 Corinthians 5:17

How were you different when you were unsaved as to now as a Christian? How was your attitude? Was the focus all on you? Unbelievers are very self-centered people. They look out for themselves and not others. They think the world revolves around them. They spend their money on themselves and collect a lot of possessions.

Hopefully, you are a Christian now. Can you see a huge difference in yourself? I've spent years collecting things and now I'm downsizing. It's just stuff. You can't take it with you. Now I can't buy anything without thinking what that money could do for Christ.

Are you a new creature in Christ? Have you given up all bad habits? What's holding you back?

June 20

Angels

Be not forgetful to entertain strangers for thereby some have entertained angels unawares.

Hebrews 13:2

In movies, it shows people walking up to other people and carrying on a conversation as if they were human. Minutes later the person suddenly disappears in thin air.

I have friends who have encountered angels. One friend was at the hospital with her dying husband. She entered his room and a woman was standing by his bed assuring him that everything was going to be all right. The woman left the room and my friend asked her husband who she was. He didn't know her name. My friend walked to the door and looked down the hall. The woman was no where to be found. My friend went to the nurse's station and asked if they knew whom the woman was that just left. They said they didn't see anyone pass the station. My friend figured out it was an angel because her husband died shortly after the encounter. The angel had come to comfort her husband. Be kind to everyone you meet. It could be an angel.

June 21

Rejoice

This is the day which the Lord hath made, we will rejoice and be glad in it.

Psalm 118:24

    I sang this song to my friend Lougenia every time I visited her. She had a massive stroke and it left her unable to speak or move. The last time I sang this song to her, she managed to wink at me. I felt like it was a thank you from God. Lougenia sang in the choir and now it was my time to sing to her. This went on for months. Not many people came to visit, but I talked to Lougenia as if nothing was wrong. I kept her up to date on all the news. I told her about my book signings and my girls. But most of all we talked about heaven. I knew God was keeping her here for a reason. Someone needed some more time with her, so they could reach a point to let her go. We have to remember God's timing is perfect. God made today so let's be glad. I'm glad I'm another day closer to heaven, my real home.

June 22

Face

Seek the Lord and His strength, seek His face continually.
1 Chronicles 16:11

    I have a sheet of paper that has some dots on it. If you stare at it for twenty seconds and then close your eyes, the image of Jesus' face will appear. It's so cool. My daughter brought it home from school one day. I've made several copies of it and passed it to friends. I'll see about putting it in the back of this book, so you can experience it, too. Don't ask me to explain how it works. The person who figured it out had to be very smart.
    I love to seek the Lord and I don't hesitate to ask for His strength. I find myself asking for His strength more and more each day. As I become more and more disabled, I become weaker. I do hope my Lord is coming soon. I'm running out of body parts! I can't wait to see His smiling face.

June 23

Free

Stand fast therefore in the liberty wherewith Christ hath made us free.
Galatians 5:1

Most of the time we don't think about being free until the 4th of July rolls around. Our day of salvation has set us free from the bondage of Satan. Do you know the date of your freedom? I know I was nine years old so I can figure out the year. I have a piece of paper taped inside my Living Bible that has my girls' baptism recorded. I cut it out of the church bulletin from that day. Our preacher baptized them in the same water, which made it very special. Nothing has made me any happier since that day. The joy of knowing that your children are saved is beyond words.

June 24

Hear

Blessed are they that hear the word of God and keep it.
Luke 11:28

I've heard the words of God since I was a very small child. I can remember reading my daily Bible verses and not understanding what I had read. The King James Version is not easy for a child to understand. Some adults have trouble with it. There are several Bibles that read more like a conversation and it's easier to understand. Just be careful about reading alternative Bibles.

If you can read and understand the word of God, then comes the next task of keeping His word. We need to apply His word in our life. It's not enough just to read it. Reading it doesn't create any action. We need to put action to His word. Loving your neighbor is nice, but it's better to show your neighbor the love. Remember we are to be the hands and feet of Christ, because He is not here to do it Himself. I could not go to Africa, but my husband went in my place and shared the love of Christ with total strangers. The people of Ghana saw Christ through the mission team. Will you go for Christ?

June 25

Shine

Let your light so shine before men, that they may see your good works, and glorify your Father which is in heaven.
                                                    Matthew 5:16

The people in Ghana saw the light of Christ in each team members' face. Thirteen Miss. State students gave up a summer of their life to go and serve Christ in a way most people wouldn't be willing to do. I admire these young people. I would like to think I would have been willing to go for Christ when I was in college. When I was fourteen, I wanted to join the Peace Core so maybe I would have gone in college had I been given the opportunity. I know these students will have some special rewards in heaven waiting on them. I hope I get to meet them some day. I can tell by the pictures that the children really enjoyed them, especially the orphans. You can go to the www.rafiki-foundation.org website and sponsor a child. There's a huge need for help with all the orphans across Africa. I'm talking about $25 a month which most of us can afford. I just sponsored twins.

June 26

Works

The Son of man shall come in the glory of His Father with His angels; and then He shall reward every man according to His works.
Matthew 16:27

Yes, Jesus will come again and I pray it is soon and very soon. Live each day as if it were your last for it very well could be. I pray your salvation is secure and your name is written in the book of life. We all need to be ready for Jesus' return.

As if getting to heaven would be enough, then we'll receive rewards for our work done here. I don't know if it'll be crowns, but whatever the reward is, I feel like we'll lay those at the foot of the throne where Jesus will be seated. I think Jesus will be the only one who is deserving of a reward because He laid down His life for us.

June 27

Now

Choose you this day whom ye will serve;...but as for me and my house, we will serve the Lord.

Joshua 24:15

I have this verse on my wall in my kitchen. I chose to serve Jesus as a child. There is no one else in the whole world who means more to me than Jesus. He has stayed with me while others have abandoned me. He has remained faithful and true while others have not.

I raised our girls in the church just like I was reared. My husband didn't come back to church until the girls were in high school. The girls attended Chrysalis while in high school and my husband and I attended Emmaus in '96. Promise Keepers and Emmaus were responsible for bringing my husband back to church. We began a couple's Sunday school class. My husband is now teaching a wonderful men's Bible study called "Authentic Manhood". We are both involved in charities at home and abroad.

My husband has just been asked to join the board of 4M Foundation and he'll be making presentations to help raise money to build more churches in Ghana, Africa. 4M also builds churches in Russia. They are currently working in Beijing, China and hopefully will be building churches in the near future there. 4M is helping establish Emmaus Walks in Russia, Honduras, and Ghana.

There's plenty of need in the world and it needs you to help. Be the hands and feet of Christ. His kingdom depends on it. See you there.

June 28

Needs

God shall supply all your needs according to His riches in glory by Christ Jesus.

Philippians 4:19

    So many people can't trust in what they can not see. The belief in God demands a great deal of trust. You will have to believe the Bible is the word of God and is nothing but the truth. I feel like this is why there aren't more Christians in this world. Most people like to be able to see and touch their God.

    My God has been there every time for me. He has not failed me. I know if I was to lose all my belongings that God would help me recover. I know He loves me beyond words. He carried me through our daughter's hospital stay for an eating disorder. He has guided my husband and me through marriage counseling, when most would have thrown in the towel. He carried me through my surgeries and all my eye problems. No matter what life throws at us, I know God will be there in the middle of it all. He can not abandon His own.

June 29

Pure Heart

Blessed are the pure in heart for they shall see God.
Matthew 5:8

There are lots of people who do things to get attention for their own glory. They like to toot their own horn. This does not make God happy. God wants His children to have pure hearts and do everything for His glory. Give everything to God and watch how much better things turn out with the Master at the wheel. God will bless you for wanting to be more like Him. Just think, some day we'll stand before Him. Wonder what He'll say first?

June 30

The Door

Behold I stand at the door, and knock: if any man hear my voice, and open the door, I will come in to him, and will sup with him, and he with me.

Revelation 3:20

Picture Jesus standing on the other side of your door to your home. He woos us to come to Him and it's up to us to open the door to our hearts. Learn to listen for His voice. You will need to learn discernment because there will be plenty of people who will try to trip you up and get you to renounce your faith. Remember Satan is like a wolf in sheep's clothing. He's constantly telling you false things to make you fall.

Jesus wants to be Lord and Master of your life. He wants to live in your heart and do all things with you. If He were here in the flesh, He would want to come see you and eat with you. He would want to go on long walks with you. Even though, He's in heaven, He can still do these things. Learn to think eternally. Try it. It's awesome.

July 1

Saved

God sent not His Son into the world to condemn the world; but that the world through Him might be saved.

John 3:17

Jesus was sent to earth for one reason and that was to be the sacrifice so the world might be saved. I just watched "The Passion of Christ" again for the fourth time and it makes me sick to see how He was beaten so badly. He was convicted of a crime He did not commit. His own people sentenced Him to death for claiming to be the Messiah. They saw the miracles, but they still did not believe. That's horrible. That tells me nothing could have convinced them, He was the Son of God. They deserved to die a horrible death for the way they treated our Lord. They knew Him. They walked with Him and still could not believe who He was. Do you know anyone who is that hardheaded about believing? I know quiet a few. I know some that believe there is a higher power, but don't believe in the Jesus and God of the Bible. I guess they think the Bible is a book of fables. Some day they will have to stand before God and it won't make any difference what they say in their defense. Their fate will be sealed. We shouldn't give up on them because as long as they have breath left in them; there's a chance for salvation.

July 2

Help

My help cometh from the Lord, which made heaven and earth.
Psalm 121:2

My Lord is the ultimate creator. There is no one anywhere that has created more or anything better. If you need help, you want the strongest, brightest, and smartest person for the job, right? Well, I know who fits that description and His name is Jesus.

Who will you ask for help, today?

July 3
Burdens

Bear ye one another's burdens, and so fulfill the law of Christ.
Galatians 6:2

Some people can't bear their own burdens much less anyone else's. Why do you think God wants us to help others with their problems? If we can't help our own friends then how are we going to help those we don't know? Helping others is what Jesus expects of us as Christians. We are to show His love to everyone we meet. After all you may be the only one who has the opportunity to show Christ to an unbeliever. If you're their only opportunity to learn about Christ and you don't help them, then you have failed them and Christ. One person can make a difference. That person needs to be you. Do something nice for someone today that hasn't asked for anything. Learn to look for needs before they are mentioned. I've had a total stranger do something nice for me without any provocation and it creates a wonderful feeling inside of you.

I bought a student's school supplies once at Walmart that was standing behind me. Boy, was he surprised. Do something nice for someone today. You'll love the blessing you receive.

July 4

Always

Lo, I am with you always, even unto the end of the world.
Matthew 28:20

This is the day that we celebrate our freedom. We have the right to worship whenever and where ever we want. This country was founded on Christianity and it's sad that we've gotten so far away from our morals. Our founders were very strict religious people. They were hard working, faithful followers of Christ. Most did not survive the harsh winters, but they never lost their faith in God. They knew they were not alone in this country. They knew that God was with them every step of the way.

No one ever said life would be easy. Matter of fact, God tells us there will be tough times. We are instructed to build our faith upon the rock for when the waters come. Who is the rock? Jesus Christ is the rock of salvation. If you believe in the Son of God, you will always have the Holy Spirit with you. The Holy Spirit will protect you, comfort you, and give you strength to face any problems you might encounter.

When you celebrate the 4th of July today, remember the freedom that comes with having Jesus Christ as your Savior. You no longer belong to this world. You belong to Christ and His kingdom, which is not here; but above. You are set free from the bondage of Satan. Thank God for freedom.

July 5

Greatness

Great is the Lord, and greatly to be praised.
1 Chronicles 16:25

There are so many ungrateful people in this world. When I hear someone who isn't appreciative of things, I tell them to check their pulse. They could be dead. There's an alternative.

People, who constantly complain, need to start a journal where they write down 4-5 things from each day that they are thankful for. You can get them started by giving them a journal and explaining what you want them to do with it. After 30 days, you should see a difference in their attitude. I've even called my friend and asked her to read to me some of the entries, just to make sure she was doing the activity. People have to be trained to look for the positive because they naturally draw to the negative.

God wants us to be thankful for everything He has done for us and has yet to do. There's always someone who has it worse than us. Be thankful for everything from the sunrise to the sunset. Be thankful you live in a free country. It could be much worse! Be thankful you live in a land of opportunity. You can be anything you want here, not so in third world countries.

God has out done Himself and we need to greatly praise Him for everything. Just wait till you get to heaven and see what He has created for just for you.

July 6

Be Still

Be still and know that I am God.

Psalm 46:10

I've had to learn this lesson and it wasn't easy. When I was told I had a tumor growing behind my eye, I wanted to have it removed right away. My insurance company said I couldn't have the surgery till I lost 66% of my vision. I thought they were playing God with my life. I didn't like having to wait, but I had no choice, because the surgery would cost over $100,000. I wasn't about to pay that amount out of my pocket, so I waited a year and a half to have my surgery. The doctor said the tumor was three weeks away from getting to my brain when He went in. That would have been terrible had it gotten on my brain. I had to learn to be still and listen to God and put all my trust and faith in Him. God blessed me with two awesome surgeons. There were some complications, but God worked them out. God had me in a tight situation where I was forced to be still and wait on Him. I hope it doesn't take something this drastic to get you to be still and know that He is in control. God is awesome!

July 7

Prayer

The effectual fervent prayer of a righteous man availeth much.
James 5:16

A righteous person has a direct line to God. When we are obedient and seeking God's will He will honor our prayers. Remember God doesn't always answer right away. God works in His time frame. He knows what's best and when it's the right time. Learn to trust in the "big" man upstairs.

It helps to keep a prayer journal. I love writing in the results. It's just more proof of what God has done. I know you've heard this before, but there's a reason for repeating it!

July 8

Merry

A merry heart doeth good like a medicine.

Proverbs 17:22

You've heard this one before, also. When you're happy the blood flows better. You will suffer less disease, when your heart is happy. You'll burn more calories, too. We could all benefit from a positive attitude. Life just flows so much better when you're happier. God desires a merry heart for you, so why not work with God on this one? Get busy.

July 9

Obey

Obey my voice, and I will be your God.

Jeremiah 7:23

Why do we have so much trouble obeying? Brides are even taking the word obey out of their wedding vows. What's going on here? People are having trouble with authority and Satan loves the "rebel" in us. He encourages us to do things on our own and forget all the rules. He loves a lawbreaker! Satan knows if you can't obey man's laws that you can't obey God's laws, either. He is so right on that one!

Do you know someone who continually breaks the law? Look closely at their attitude. They were probably not taught as a child to respect authority or made to mind their parents coming up. This is a fatal mistake for parents. God has instructed parents to raise their children right. It's the parents' responsibility to teach their children how to respect others and the law. So many parents are trying to be their children's best friend. You can't do that. You are the person in charge, not one of the guys. Raise your children by God's laws and you'll be proud of your children and how they turned out. Mine are not perfect, but I am proud of who they have become. There is always room for improvement with all of us. You can set the example.

July 10

Light

I am come a light into the world, that whosoever believeth on me should not abide in darkness.

John 12:46

I was just watching the film on the 15 hostages that were held in Columbia. There were three U.S. military contractors in the group and they were held for 5 years. Some of the others were held for as much as 10 years. The Columbian Government said no ransom was paid for their release. The government trained three people to pretend they were part of the rebel group and were suppose to transport the hostages to another location. After the plane took off, the hostages were told they were free. They were extremely happy.

This is the way we should feel because Christ came into a dark world and offered Himself for the sacrifice for our sins. We have paid nothing. Jesus paid it all! We will never live in darkness again because of the light of the world that now lives within us. Amen!

July 11

Peace

The Lord will give strength unto His people; the Lord will bless His people with peace.

Psalm 29:11

How about some more peace? We're going to need it as the world spins toward its final end. Thank goodness, God will protect us with all the crazy things going on around us. Everywhere you turn terrorists are trying to plant bombs. Let's face facts. The terrorists are not going away. These are people who are willing to give up their life for their cause. Are we Christians willing to lay down our lives for Christ? The apostles did just that. If the apostles had not been so dedicated to spreading the word, we might not have ever heard of Christianity. The apostles considered it a privilege to suffer as Jesus suffered for us. They were considered outlaws of religion. When they were told to stop preaching, they continued and some were thrown in jail, some were stoned and some were crucified.

If you want to learn more about these great men, watch "The Story of the Twelve Apostles". They started out as fishermen, farmers, and local magistrates; but because of their love for Jesus, they changed the world in ways that would spread across time, spanning over two thousand years.

July 12

Pleasure

It is your father's good pleasure to give you the kingdom.
                                                    Luke 12:32

You have an idea how it feels to give someone you love a really nice gift. Well, Jesus can top that feeling! He handed you His kingdom when you accepted Him as your Savior. We don't deserve any of it, but it was paid for with a very high price; while being free to you. You'll never receive a gift as valuable as that as long as you live. How often do you thank God? It should be a daily event. If you need help remembering, write it in red on your calendar. Write it on a piece of paper and tape it to your mirror. Whatever it takes, learn to thank God for what He has done for you. Don't complain about what you don't have. Don't compare yourself to your family members or friends. Remember it's harder for a rich person to get into heaven, than it is for a camel to make it through the eye of a needle. I look at the Donald Trumps and Oprahs of the world and I would not want to trade places. Money can not buy happiness. Ask the lottery winners and they'll tell you the truth!

July 13

Everlasting

The eternal God is thy refuge, and underneath are the everlasting arms.
Deuteronomy 33:27

    This verse makes me think of the circus performers when they don't have a net under them. Thank goodness, I have God's everlasting arms to catch me when I fall. God never gets tired of catching us or picking us up after a fall. This also reminds me of when my girls were little and I had to pick them up and kiss their bobos. It's the same kind of love but on a grander scale. Hopefully, you still comfort your children even if they are grown. They will always need us, just like we'll always need God's help in everything we do. He taught mothers how to nurture. Learn from the Master.

July 14

Rest

Rest in the Lord, and wait patiently for Him.
Psalm 37:7

Unfortunately, we are wound a little too tight. We live in a very fast pace world where only the strong survive. It's a dog-eat-dog world. I'm so glad, I'm out of the rat race of life, but not happy to be disabled. I work for Christ and I've got all the time in the world. No deadlines, no one standing over me, no co-harts to deal with, no need to rush out the door, no traffic to deal with, and no clock to punch. I still have to deal with high pressure. It's genetic. It is called hypertension and I inherited it from my father. My driving days are numbered and that's good for the public and myself. I've already been in eight wrecks and that alone will take a toll on the body. I'm learning to rest in the Lord and it's wonderful! I'm also learning patience. Patience is an emotion that is learned. It's probably one of the hardest to develop. Remember all things are possible through Christ. So there's hope for us!

July 15

Humble

Humble yourselves in the sight of the Lord, and He shall lift you up.
James 4:10

Humility is a necessity for a true Christian. It's also another difficult emotion to learn. You are not born with it. My mother set a wonderful example for me, but look at how humble Jesus was. He spoke with the most gentle, kind voice. His words spill like honey all over you. His touch healed people instantly. He cared for all, not just a select few. He loves you, even though you've never laid eyes on Him. He has known you since birth and can call you by name. Do you call on Him?

No matter how down you may be, Jesus can lift you up to new heights. Don't look to mankind to lift you up. Most will just step over you. Call on the one that is the most dependable. Seek out other Christian friends who care enough to help you up and dust you off. God made friends as life preservers. Select them carefully.

July 16

Only One

There is one God; and there is none other but He.

Mark 12:32

Here's a verse that you need to memorize so when others from different religions question you; you will be able to quote God with these exact words. Pray these words will pierce the hearts of the lost.

They may not realize it, but a lost soul is always seeking the truth. It's how God designed us. We're born with an innate sense of a higher power. I pray that when they hear the truth their hearts will leap and realize these words are straight from God above.

You can't worship God and have any other idols. An idol can be something or someone that you give more value to than God Himself. God has to be number one in your life. Don't let your money, kids, pets, or anything else come before God.

July 17

Pray

Rejoice evermore. Pray without ceasing.
1 Thessalonians 5:16-17

There has never been a day to go by where there was nothing to pray about. When you get my age, you'll experience a lot of sleepless nights. I use them wisely. I start with family and after they are covered, I move to all my friends. Last but not least, I pray for those whose loved ones have asked for prayer. At some point, I will finally fall asleep or not. I know half of the world is asleep but God never sleeps. Amen! Someone somewhere needs your prayers. Paul instructed us to never stop praying. This is so true. We can't afford to take a break, because the evil one never rests. He is devouring people like a lion. He's going to have a lot of company in that lake of fire. Right now there is around six billion people in the world. If you took a head count right now, I doubt there would be even close to one billion saved. That's just an estimated guess based on the percentage of Christians known today. Famous people, rich people, kings, royalty, heads of state, and so forth will be found in hell.

Live your life so when you put your foot on the floor, Satan will say, "Oh, no! She's up!"

July 18

Joy

Sorrow is turned into joy before Him.

Job 41:22

    Here's a promise we all need to claim. God promises to turn all your sorrow into joy. Notice there's no time frame mentioned here, but it's the end result that matters. There is a time to grieve and there is a time to rejoice. There are five stages of grief and we move through those stages at different paces. Some even go back and forth between some of the phases. I wouldn't pay too much attention to the different phases unless you've gotten stuck in one for too long a time. I grieved over my mother for 18 years and that was too long. I put a lot of time and energy into my relationship with my mom and when she was gone, I was devastated. I could not be consoled. I needed professional help, but back then we didn't have it available in the small town where I lived. It was years later before I received help.

    We don't live forever here and thank goodness people aren't living to be 800-900 years old anymore. Can you imagine trying to remember events in your life, when you've lived that long? I have trouble now. That's something to add to your thankful list!

July 19

Knee Mail

The Lord upholdeth all that fall, and raiseth up all those that be bowed down.

Psalm 145:14

People talk about their emails, text messages, and so on; but what's more important than all of those put together? Knee mail! People that spend most of their time on their knees will have no trouble standing in time of crisis. God will see to it that you are given the strength that you need. Bow down before Him and cry out His name. He has perfect hearing. He has supernatural powers. He puts all the super heroes to shame. Some day we'll get to see it up close and personal. Be exceedingly glad that you can call Him, Father.

July 20

Removed

> *As far as the east is from the west, so far hath He removed our transgressions from us.*
>
> *Psalm 103:12*

I love this verse! When we ask God for forgiveness with a sincere heart, then and only then are our sins removed. Amen! We've all made mistakes and I'm so glad that God has chosen to erase them. If our friends and families could do this, it would be great. Remember God is not human. We tend to hold on to grudges and want to collect them like we collect stamps. When something happens, we'll pull out our grudges and beat our loved ones over the head again and again, like a broken record. We naturally want to punish people who have wronged us. Forgive them and move forward. Remember God is the judge. He's not going to let anyone get away with anything. Give it to God and trust Him to handle it for you.

July 21

Intercession

We know not what we should pray for...but the Spirit itself maketh intercession for us.

Romans 8:26

Isn't it great that the Holy Spirit does so much for us, especially things we're not equipped to do? That's awesome. People have reported unusual strength in rare cases, feelings of a presence, like an angel, sightings of loved ones that have passed on and etc.

If no one is praying for you or you're not able, the Holy Spirit is praying for you on your behalf. You are covered. I think our loved ones are also praying for us in heaven. Jesus makes His request known to the Father and I can't see God refusing His request. Give thanks for intercession!

July 22

Teach

Teach me thy way, O Lord, and lead me in a plain path.

Psalm 27:11

This was a request to God that He explain in an understanding manner what He expects us to do. Let there be a line of honest communication between us and God, so there will be no confusion on our part. We need to walk in confidence without hesitation, because there are observers waiting for a stumble or fall from grace.

Peter's faith wavered more than any other apostle, but He became the leader of the group after Jesus' death. That's why he became known as the "rock". He became what God designed him to be. Are you the person that you were created to be by God? If not, I pray you are well on your way. God needs you!

July 23

Charity

Charity...beareth all things, believeth all things, hopeth all things, endureth all things.

1 Corinthians 13:4,7

    We as Christians are expected to be servants of God. We're studying service in Vacation Bible School this month. I've got the second lesson to teach which is on friends. I will tell the story about the four friends that carried their parallelized friend to see Jesus. They cut a hole in the roof of the house where Jesus was speaking and lowered their friend down in front of Him. What did Jesus do? Jesus told the man to get up and go. Jesus never laid a hand on him, but spoke the command and the man believeth and so it was. This man had never seen Jesus before, but he had heard of His healings. His friends cared enough to take him to Jesus. They didn't let the crowd stop them. I wonder how the homeowner felt when he saw them cutting through his roof. I hope they willingly helped repair the roof. It wouldn't be very Christian of them if they didn't. It's great to have that kind of friends. Even though, He's not physically with us now, you can lift up your friends to Jesus through prayer. The prayers of friends are powerful!

July 24

Blessed

Blessed is the man that endureth temptations: for...he shall receive the crown of life, which the Lord hath promised to them that love Him.

James 1:12

It's not a sin to be tempted. It's a sin to give in to Satan. We're tempted all the time. Satan is hoping we'll take the bait. Ask God to give you the strength to resist when temptation comes calling. I have a placemat I make for Emmaus Walks that says, "When Satan calls, let God answer." He will do that for you. Just ask.

I have a card I make that says, "Try Jesus. If you don't like Him, Satan will always take you back." One more saying, "Don't give Satan a ride, he always wants to drive." If Satan gets a hold on you, God is the only one who can break the chains of bondage.

July 25

Created

We are His workmanship, created in Christ Jesus unto good works.
Ephesians 2:10

    We were created to do good, not evil. Thank goodness we weren't created like robots, but with free will. How would you feel if your children or pets came to you because they had to? When they come out of love it feels really good. That's how God feels when you come to Him because you love Him. He's a proud Father. When His children obey and want to do good works in His name; He is busting all over with joy. Just remember to give God credit and praise in all that you do.

July 26

Give

It is more blessed to give than to receive.

Acts 20:35

    I learned this one early. I've always been a giver. I was always the one to send birthday cards, call, and give gifts for no reason. Over the years, I've had to cut back on the gifts because I no longer work. There are also other acts of kindness that you can't put a price on. Helping young mothers out with some babysitting is huge. Sitting with someone in the hospital is another one. When I have surgery, my girls stay with me so my husband can go home and take care of my dogs. I rest better knowing someone is looking after my babies. They are very precious to me.

    There are hundreds of other acts of kindness so I'm sure you'll be able to come up with some on your own. Start today. Start with your immediate family and come up with something that will serve each member in a very special way. Spread out from there and serve your friends next. The ultimate test is to do something for a total stranger. Please don't expect anything in return. Give freely.

July 27

Faith

If ye have faith as a grain of mustard seed,...nothing shall be impossible unto you.

Matthew 17:20

    I want you to find a mustard seed and put it where you can see it daily. I want you to repeat this verse for 30 days straight. It takes that long to break a bad habit. So I figure it will take that long to convince you that nothing is impossible for God; if you have the faith the size of a mustard seed. That's not much. Mustard seeds are very small.

    Ask a man who has had a kidney stone the size of a mustard seed, how much pain he was in. You won't believe the pain that it causes. It may be small, but when it comes to kidney stones; it'll stop you in your tracks. I had one the size of my thumbnail and thought I would die!

July 28

Chosen

God hath from the beginning chosen you to salvation through sanctification of the Spirit and belief of the truth.

2 Thessalonians 2:13

That's right! You were chosen from the beginning to belong to God. He called your name and hopefully, you answered that call. Some just ignore the call and do whatever they want. Some day they'll wish they had answered God's call. They will have to stand before God and acknowledge Him before they are sentenced to hell. They will know then what a mistake they have made and there won't be anything they can do to change it.

I was watching the movie " The Gospel of John" and I wish I had counted how many times Jesus said the word truth. People kept asking Him, "What is the truth?" When Jesus explained to them that He was the Son of God, they didn't believe Him. I would like to know how many conversions were made right after the crucifixion. I bet they felt real sick when they realized they had killed God's only Son. They killed an innocent man.

July 29

New Day

His compassions fail not. They are new every morning: great is thy faithfulness.

Lamentations 3:22-23

Sometimes our families and friends aren't there for us. Not the case with Jesus! This verse says, He will never be put off by us or tire of our complaining. He'll always be there every day, so start your morning off with Him. He'll always be there for us. He promises to be there every day. He is faithful to complete a good work in you till the day He takes you home to be with Him. Amen!

Today is the first day of the rest of your life.

July 30

Tall Task

Love your enemies, bless them that cuss you, do good to them that hate you, and pray for them which despitefully use you.
Matthew 5:44

This is very hard for everyone, not just a few. God is the only one that requires us to love our enemies. I don't know any other God out there that asks its followers to do this. I know some that demand that they hate infantiles and create jihad against anyone who does not belong to their religion.

We are not to hate anyone. After 911, it would be extremely hard not to hate the attackers. They took out so many innocent people that day.

I've been used before and it's not a good feeling. It takes the awesome power of God to help you get past this kind of deceit. I like to think the best of everyone, but I'm not stupid.

I know I have people that hate me, but that's their problem; not mine. I was brought up not to hate anyone, but it was my stepmother who made it easy to hate her. I had to ask God to help me forgive her. I couldn't have done it without His help. Now, I won't allow myself to fall into that trap set by Satan. Ask God to help you rise above the evil. Don't lower yourself into the hands of Satan.

July 31

Foolishness

The foolishness of God is wiser than men; and the weakness of God is stronger than men.

1 Corinthians 1:25

We as humans do some pretty stupid things. I wonder if God thinks it's funny when we make fools of ourselves? I can't imagine any foolishness coming from God and I have a pretty active imagination. I think Paul was trying to make a point of how smart God really is. His strength is stronger than the world. Remember the song, "He's Got The Whole World In His Hands"? He can really hold it all. Then why don't more give their burdens to Him?

August 1

Follow

And he said to them all, "If any man will come after me, let him deny himself, and take up his cross daily and follow me."

Luke 9:23

    The apostles were the first to follow Jesus. I don't know what criteria He used in selecting them, but I'm sure He had a method. He chose ordinary men to do unspeakable tasks. They were a little slow in figuring out who He was, in my opinion; but the end results were what mattered. They scattered after Jesus' death, but fifty days later, Jesus visited them and brought them back together. They were sent out to heal the sick and preach the good news and then they reported back to Jesus. They were ecstatic over how well they were received. Now, it was time for Jesus to tell them He was leaving for good. They would be on their own, but the day of Pentecost came and the Holy Spirit was given to each of them. The Holy Spirit went with them and they were able to speak whatever language was spoken in the country where they were. If the apostles had not been willing to go for Christ, then Christianity might have died. There was no way God would have let that happen.

    God is counting on you and me to help spread the word. We have to do what we can while there is still time. Time is growing short. Time will run out for some today.

August 2

Why

When we know who, we can stop asking why.
                                            Dr. David Jeremiah

I don't always get to hear Dr. Jeremiah on Sunday mornings, but I love his style of preaching. He has a simple deliverance with his message and he keeps it simple enough for others to understand. Not everyone is educated, so it's important to keep the message on a level for most to understand. If you preach over their IQ level, then you might as well go home. You have defeated your purpose.

My degree is in elementary education so I'm not going to test your knowledge with some four and five-dollar words to show you how smart I am.

Salvation is all about who you know. Jesus is His name. Who was Jesus? He was the Son of God sent to save the world. That's the most important message in the Bible. If you don't get anything else, get this! Memorize John 3:16 and don't ever forget it. You may need to quote it some day to a lost soul and won't have your Bible handy. You may have to recite it some day to a dying person. Their life could depend on it!

August 3
High Ground

When faced with a swamp, look for the high ground to make your way across.

Dr. David Jeremiah

I love this saying by Dr. Jeremiah. This one is worth making a sign to post somewhere in your home. We all know who the high ground is. There is none higher than God. Some days you may feel like you're in it up to your neck, but God has the power to make it all go away.

There's a swampy area north of Senatobia along the 51 highway and I can't stand to look at it as I drive by. I have to keep my one eye focused on my lane so I won't end up in the swamp. From time to time, people have run off into the swamp and that's never good. It looks real snaky.

When you find yourself in the swamps of life, it's good to have a lifeline. You're going to need the best. Remember Jesus saves!

August 4

Praise

When you can't see God in your problems, you'll see Him in your praise.

Dr. David Jeremiah

I guess this quote is like, when you can't see the forest for the trees statement. Some are so upset over the problems that they can't see the bigger picture. God is there right in the middle of everything. He didn't walk out on you. Check your focus.

I've seen people standing in what was left of their home, praising God, that they were still alive. They may have lost all their possessions, but they came through the storm with their life. Amen! That's the sign of a true Christian. They knew He could have taken them out and they were thankful to live another day. God giveth and God taketh away. It's His decision to make. Without the storm, we can not have a rainbow.

August 5

Who

Who am I, O Lord God...that you have brought me this far?
2 Samuel 7:18

I wish I knew how many times I've asked God that one. I've been in eight wrecks, two tornadoes, a fire, and a flood.

Throw in a few small hurricanes, too. I've even experienced a few small earthquakes. I live near the New Madrid Fault, so we're suppose to get the "big one" some day. I hope I'm out of here when that happens.

Why has God brought any of us this far? We were created to fellowship with Him and there have been some days where I wanted to ask Him, if we were having fun, yet?

I know He has to be very sad over the state of the world. It makes me sad! How much is enough? He wiped Sodom and Gomorrah off the map.

What if the terrorists disable our country to the point it throws us into a deep depression? I think we fell asleep at the wheel when we continued to let people enter our borders. Terrorists are in this country right now planning attacks. Why aren't we seeking them out and sending them back to their own country? Some day we'll be sorry we didn't pay better attention to what was going on right under our noses. We need to be vigilant. Remember the soldiers that David picked to be in his army? He picked the ones who drank with one hand while watching over their shoulders. He won the battle with a small number of men. He picked the best.

August 6

Faith

Without faith it is impossible to please Him.

Hebrews 11:6

You probably know how it feels when someone doesn't have enough faith in you. It's not a good feeling. Here God is telling you to have faith in Him. There is nothing He can't do, so why would you doubt Him?

I grew up not being able to trust men, so I understand why some might have a problem with trust. I had to get past the fact, that Jesus and God are both men. If you've been abused, just remember Jesus and God are holy and they can't sin against you like man. They are not liars. They have no evil intent toward you. They are the only men you can really trust without a shadow of doubt. Evil men will lie to you, steal from you, and abandon you. It's imperative to find a good upstanding man of God. If you can't find one, make do with Jesus and God. They are all that you need, anyway. You'll find none better.

August 7

Forgiveness

Do not judge and you will not be judged. Do not condemn, and you will not be condemned. Forgive, and you will be forgiven.
Luke 6:37

Talk about a hard request from God. We naturally want to judge everybody and everything we see. I judge the beauty pageant at the fair in Tate County, which is okay. What God is talking about here are other kinds of judgmental thoughts toward others. Judging someone for his or her actions or clothes that they wear is not right. God didn't appoint us to be judge and jury of anyone. When we are called to serve on a jury of law, we have to report and fulfill our duty as a citizen. That's what our law requires of us. God expects us to abide by our laws.

God is asking us not to condemn someone to hell, but pray for the person, instead. I have a real hard time with sexual predators. I have no mercy for someone who harms a child. I turn them over to God for Him to decide what needs to be done to them. If you were a sexual predator, you would not want me on the throne, deciding your fate!

In order for us to receive our forgiveness, we must first forgive those who have harmed us. He's a tough Father, isn't He? Remember, He knows best.

August 8

Wishes

The Lord is near all who call out to Him, all who call out to Him with integrity. He fulfills the desires of those who fear Him; He hears their cry for help and saves them.
Psalm 145:18-19

I'm so thankful that God is always near. Can you imagine having to wait for Him to get there in a time of need?

We don't have to call 911 for Him to respond. Just call out His name and He promises to hear your cry. When you were a child, did you ever have to call for your parents in the middle of the night? I didn't, because I slept in the same room as my parents and I'm so thankful for that security. I needed it. At the time, I may not have appreciated not having my own room; but I learned later why that was the best place for me to be. My parents had no clue what evil lived inside the walls of our home. Things aren't always, as they seem. Be watchful!

August 9

Confidence

I am able to do all things through Him who strengthens me.
Philippians 4:13

People have been given extraordinary strength through the power of the Holy Spirit. Look at the apostles. They were given the same healing power that Jesus had. Well, guess what? We have the same Holy Spirit inside of us. If you believe you can do all things through Christ, then you can.

Next time you're faced with a difficult situation, call on the Holy Spirit and see what happens. If you ask for help, He'll give it to you. He's not going to deny His child of help. God loves you!

August 10

God's Best

In your presence is abundant joy; in your right hand are eternal pleasures.

Psalm 16:11

We were talking today about eternal things and someone said they hoped there would be plenty of food in heaven. She was tired of having to walk off her calories. Amen! I know there will be food because the Bible says we'll have a feast. You can't have a feast without food. I don't know what kind of food we'll have, but who cares?

Why is the right hand mentioned? The right hand is a place of honor because that's where Jesus sits. You will be given eternal pleasure because God holds you in a place of honor.

How many people do you think misses the abundant joy? If you don't acknowledge it, then you can't claim it. It's true. Wouldn't you rather have joy over sadness? What's keeping you from being happy? Be happy!

August 11

God's Love

Your love has delivered me from the pit of destruction, for you have thrown all my sins behind your back.

Isaiah 38:17

Amen! I use to live in fear of some day getting to heaven and all my sins would be on a huge screen for all to see. Well, I'm not going to stand before the throne of judgment because Jesus Christ died for my sins. I have confessed my sins and they are gone forever. Amen!

It's the unbelievers who will stand before God and answer for their sins. They won't have any excuses good enough to save them. God will remind them of the opportunities they rejected. It was their choice not to follow Christ. They will get exactly what they deserve.

Thank you, God for sending your Son to save us! Thank you! Thank you! Thank you!

August 12

Empitness

Now may the God of hope fill you with all joy and peace in believing, so that you may overflow with hope by the power of the Holy Spirit.
Romans 15:13

    The Holy Spirit can do anything so why not ask for all the joy and peace the Lord has to offer. How many people do you see on a daily basis that is overflowing with hope? Not many!

    Maybe we need to set the example of what hope looks like. Let's try something. Let's smile really "big" for thirty days and see how many people ask us why we are smiling. Your answer can be, "I have hope of a better tomorrow through Jesus Christ." I'm going to hope that we don't go through a single day without being noticed. You will learn how powerful a smile can be.

    I wear an eye patch and you wouldn't believe how many people it draws to me. I have a glass eye but it hurts to wear it, so most of the time I don't wear it. When they realize it's not temporary, their face drops. Here's an opportunity to tell them that God holds me in His hands. Besides, I'll have two eyes in eternity. They always remark that I have a good attitude about my loss. God allows things for a reason. I'm living proof. I'm turning my loss into a positive. What is your loss and what are you going to do about it?

August 13

Choices

I have set before you life and death, blessing, and curse. Choose life so that you and your descendants may live.

Deuteronomy 30:19

    Remember when Eve told Satan in the garden if she ate from the tree of knowledge that she would die? Breaking God's laws is sin and sin separates us from God, creating death. Eve didn't die a physical death but they were kicked out of the garden and away from God. We have a choice. You can obey God's laws or not. You see where it got Eve. I pray you have chosen Jesus. I pray you choose blessings over curses. I pray you have chosen life, not death. If you've chosen life, I'll see you on the other side.

August 14

Holiness

Let us draw near with a true heart in full assurance of faith, our hearts sprinkled clean from an evil conscience and our bodies washed in pure water.

Hebrews 10:22

Notice the key word "true" heart. God knows our heart so don't think you're going to put on a good front at church and walk out the door and live your life as you wish. That won't work, but there are millions doing it. They'll find out sooner or later the price for that false front.

We are instructed to clean our hearts and minds from evil. Remember the Holy Spirit can not live side by side with evil. It says to wash our bodies in pure water. Who is the pure water? Jesus. Let Jesus cleanse you from head to toe and walk in His righteousness.

August 15

Accusation

No weapon formed against you will succeed, and you will refute any accusation raised against you in court. This is the heritage of the Lord's servants, and their righteousness is from me.
                                                               Isaiah 54:17

Now, here's a comforting thought. Any of us could find ourselves in court. I accidentally hit a woman walking in a parking lot, with my car. The woman walked out in front of me and I didn't have time to stop. I felt so bad! Thank goodness, she had no broken bones and my insurance company paid her money for her suffering. It could have easily ended up in court. I praise God for watching over the woman and me.

Notice, it says, this protection is the heritage of the Lord's servants. We have an insurance policy with God because we belong to Him. He protects His own. That alone should make your day.

August 16

Warfare

You do not have to fight this battle. Position yourselves, stand still, and see the salvation of the Lord.

2 Chronicles 20:17

Here's another verse that states how God protects us from the world. We don't have to fight our own battles. He'll do it for us.

We need to stand firm, stand on the word of God, and let God do His thing. We put on the armor of God by studying His word and memorizing verses and storing them in our hearts.

I've been through a lot of trials and tribulations and God has carried me through them all. He'll do the same for you. Thank your all, loving and all protecting God for what He has done for you and what He has yet to do.

Thank you, Father!

August 17

Security

You have put more joy in my heart than they have when their grain and new wine abound. I will both lie down and sleep in peace for you alone, make me live in safety.

Psalm 4:7-8

Here's a verse that means so much in today's time. There were wars in the Bible days, but they didn't have nuclear bombs. Safety has become a hot topic for everyone, no matter, where you live. We're spending billions of dollars on homeland security and it's still not enough.

Have you noticed that we're fighting in a country that once was the home of the Garden of Eden? I don't know what the significance is, but I'm sure there's a reason why we're there. Maybe we've come full circle. Maybe we're nearing the end.

David is expressing his joy for the Lord. David was on the run from people who wanted him dead. David is praising the Lord for allowing him to sleep in peace and keeping him safe. We should do the same. God is still in control and there's no fear of Him being dethroned. This battle has already been won! You are on the winning team. If you've given your life to Christ, man can't take that away from you. Is your eternal life secure? If it's not, you can secure it today.

August 18

Forgiveness

Put on heart felt compassion, kindness, humility, gentleness, and patience, accepting one another and forgiving one another if anyone has a complaint against another.

Colossians 3:12-13

God wants us to be a good example of Him. Here's a list of what God expects from us. Compassion can be taught, but one must have a caring heart to carry it off. Kindness seems to be going by the wayside with so many people. People are not controlling their tongues. We see more and more road rage, today. Humility is also another trait that few possess. We are not better than anyone else and we need to remember that.

Gentleness is what I remember Jesus using with everyone He met especially children. We need to be careful of the words we use. They can be very hurtful. Patience has been extremely hard for me to learn and I've had some tough lessons that have made a difference in my life. Patience will serve you well, if you make up your mind that's what you're going to learn.

Accepting one another is so hard, especially for today's youth. I've worked with them, so I know this to be true. We are more alike than we are different.

Forgiveness is hard for everyone. God has helped me in this area. He will not fail you because He wants this for you. It will do you wonders!

August 19

Daily Trust

I have not departed from the commands of His lips; I have treasured the words of His mouth more than my daily food.

Job 23:12

If anyone had a reason to turn against God, it was Job. Job loved God beyond measure. Job grieved for a while and his friends couldn't even console him. Poor Job lost everything but his wife.

Job refused to give up. He continued to obey God's commands and he was rewarded greatly. Job was given a test and he passed.

Are you going through a trial or tribulation, now? Do what Job did and continue to praise God. You'll come out of this stronger on the other side. You'll also be restored!

August 20

God's Faithfulness

God is not a man who lies, or a son of man who changes His mind. Does He speak and not act or promise and not fulfill?

Numbers 23:19

This confirms what I've been telling you for the past seven months. God is holy and can not lie to you. If God promises you he'll never leave you, He means it. God speaks nothing but the truth.

The Bible is God's word and you can trust it to be the absolute truth. Spend a lot of time in His word because there will be plenty who will try to derail you off the right path. Stay true to God's word.

August 21

Victory

May you be strengthened with all power, according to His glorious might.

Colossians 1:11

Today will require a lot of strength so ask God to help you before you head for the door. Pick a verse and write it on a piece of paper and place it in your pocket. Just knowing that you have God's word in your pocket will give you strength. Try picturing Him in the car with you on your way to work. If you have a long commute, that's a good time to listen to tapes or religious music or just praying. In other words, surround and amerce yourself with the glory of God and you'll have a better day. I promise.

August 22

Endurance

The testing of your faith produces endurance. But endurance must do its complete work, so that you may be mature and complete, lacking nothing.

James 1:3-4

Why do we need to be tested? It's not for God's benefit, He already knows everything about us. I think it's for our benefit so we can learn more about God. During a challenge, we realize the strength of God. We realize we need Him and we can't cope without Him. During my lowest points, I've realized the presence of God and how much He loves me. That's huge in my book. I needed to know that he was there with me in ICU, especially since I got limited time with my husband. Tiffany sat with her dad in the waiting room, but declined to come see me in ICU. She doesn't have a strong stomach. She was excused.

After each and every trial, I've realized how faithful God is to me. Now, I know without a doubt, He's always there for me. He has given me the confidence to face each day no matter what life throws at me. I'm facing a situation where I can go blind, but with God by my side; I'm not going to waste any time worrying about it. If it happens, God will help me deal with it. Worrying has never accomplished anything.

August 23

Prayer

God is able to make every grace overflow to you, so that in every way, always having everything you need, you may excel in every good work.
2 Corinthians 9:8

God will provide all your needs. There's a lot of difference between wants and needs, so spend some time separating the two, so you can petition God for your needs. So many people are afraid to ask God for something. There's no need for you to fear Him. He loves you!

I've been criticized for doing mission work. How can someone complain how you spend your time and money? I know I'm doing what God wants me to do, so I have to let what others say roll off my back. I have to answer to God. God is working through me to help supply the poor and needy, their needs. Much is expected of those who have been given much. Where are you on this scale?

August 24

God's Love

Lord, your faithful love reaches to heaven, your faithfulness to the skies, your righteousness is like the highest mountain; your judgments like the deepest sea.

Psalm 36:5-6

This verse reminds me of the song that said, "Ain't no mountain high enough, ain't no valley low enough to keep me from you." The same is with God's love. God has enough love to fill the world several times over and then some. Who loves you, baby? God!

God loves you, whether you like it or not. That's what I tell the prisoners. They think they are so tough and say they could care less if anyone loves them. Regardless of how they feel God still loves them. There's nothing you can do to make God stop loving you. He's going to love you forever.

August 25

Suffering

Jesus said to her, "Didn't I tell you that if you believed you would see the glory of God?"

John 11:40

Once a person believes their ability to understand changes. The scriptures suddenly become clear and now they make sense. Unbelievers have blinders on until they make the decision to follow Christ. Christ opens their eyes and ears so that they will understand. When witnessing to the lost, don't bombard them with a lot of scripture. I focus on how much God loves them. John 3:16 is a perfect verse to use. Once they are saved, they will have plenty of time to study God's word. Let God speak to them on what they need to change in their lives. If you point out these problems, you'll look judgmental. You help bring them to Christ and He'll clean them up.

August 26

Peace

The Lord bless you and keep you; the Lord make His face shine up on you and be gracious to you; the Lord turn His face toward you and give you peace.

Numbers 6:24-26

I've heard this verse many times in my life. Sometimes people quote it when someone is leaving. It is an excellent blessing. It's what every parent should wish for his or her children.

You would really have to love someone with your whole heart to wish that God keep them close and have His radiant face shine on them. That's an awesome request. I would like to hear this verse daily. Maybe I should teach it to my husband. If we're blessed enough to ever have grandchildren, this is something I need to memorize. Think of the impact it would make in a young life. Maybe you have a friend or co-hart that needs to hear it on a daily basis. It's worth trying. This verse is my wish for you!

August 27

Rescue

As for me, I will look to the Lord; I will wait for the God of my salvation.

Micah 7:7

I just shared in Sunday school how I've refused to give up on a situation that I've been praying over for years. God's hands were tied to a certain extent because of our free will; but I knew God could help. I begged God to do whatever He could to touch the heart of this person. I can see God's hands at work, now. So if you have something that you want to turn over to God, don't give up. God works in another time zone from us. As long as the end results is what you've been praying about, then the time shouldn't matter. Even if you think, you'll not live long enough to see the results; still pray. Tell God you will wait, no matter, how long it takes!

August 28

Restoration

Return to your fortress, you prisoners who have hope; today I declare that I will restore double to you.

Zechariah 9:12

    Job is the expert on double restoration. I'm going to interview him when I get to heaven. He's on my list of several people that I want to talk to. Who do you want to meet, beside Christ Jesus and God?
    What ever happens to you, it helps to know that God will restore us. I've never lost all my belongings, but I've been emotionally bankrupt before. God has restored me way beyond my wildest dreams. We don't own very expensive things. I treasure my dogs over any furniture or collectibles. We can always go buy more clothes, furniture, and household items. It's just stuff!

August 29

Blessing

Blessed be the God and Father of our Lord Jesus Christ, who has blessed us with every spiritual blessing in the heavens, in Christ.

Ephesians 1:3

Could you sacrifice a child for the world to be saved? I doubt it. I know I couldn't have. That's exactly what God did! He sent His only Son to earth to die a terrible death just for you and me. God loves us that much.

Your Father loves you. Maybe you didn't have a good earthly father, or possibly you never knew your father; but your heavenly Father adores you! I want you to write down all the blessings that God has sent to you. I think you'll be surprised at how many there are. You have a Father that is a King!

August 30

Victory

People cry out because of severe oppression; they shout for help from the arm of the mighty.

Job 35:9

All you have to do is turn on the television and you'll see and hear the oppressed. People being flooded out, homes burned to the ground, homes flattened from tornadoes and so forth. The worst cries I witnessed were from hurricane Katrina. Top officials and the government made so many mistakes. You can't put people in a wide span roof building. That's a no-no! The people should have been loaded in buses and carried out of the city. People won't be allowed to stay next time.

I use to live in New Orleans and it sits below sea level. I lived in Kenner not far from the lake. There were plenty of warnings from the weather experts that New Orleans was a ticking time bomb. Well, their luck ran out.

Who did people cry out to? Some cried to the cameras, while others cried out to the military. Who is your help in time of need? God? God created this world and he controls it. Remember this verse and the mighty arm of God next time.

August 31

Live

Because you died for me, I'll live the rest of my life for you.
Vera Gaines

I made this commitment several years ago to God. He has done so much for me, the least I can do is live for Him. He has rescued me from some mighty storms and a few times He had to carry me, when I couldn't put one foot in front of the other. There was one set of footprints in the sand.

I saw a saying recently that said, "Write your sorrows in sand and write your blessings in stone." That is a perfect thing for us to do. God will take those sorrows and they will disappear, but keep a record of the blessings; so you won't forget what God has done for you.

September 1

Reconfirm

Ask God to reconfirm our understanding of His will to make things clear.

Vera Gaines

For years, I kept asking God, "Why am I here?" We've all asked that question. If you don't know by now, then keep seeking His purpose for you. We were all born for a reason.

If you haven't read, <u>The Purpose Driven Life</u> by Rick Warren, then I suggest you check it out of the library or purchase it for yourself. I bought ten copies and gave them all away. It's a wonderful book. I had already found my purpose, but I still enjoyed the book, because it confirmed my purpose. Ask God to make things so clear for you, that there will be no mistake in your interpretation. Seek God's will not your own.

September 2

Buy

Buy- and do not sell- truth, wisdom, instruction, and understanding.
Proverbs 23:23

We all need the truth because there's so much evil out there that wants us to follow the wrong path. Stay on the straight and narrow path if you want to serve God.

Wisdom comes with experience. That's why older people have more wisdom than the younger crowd. You get wisdom by studying God's word and applying it to life.

Instruction is God's word to lead, guide, and direct us through this world. God knew we would need it, so He left His word in the form of the Bible.

You have to work at understanding. It just doesn't come to you. I ask God to help me to understand what he needs to tell me. He wants you to understand, so don't hold back. Ask God for His help.

This verse says to buy these things, don't sell them. In order to sell something, you have to receive money for it and you then give it away. God says don't sell. Offer your help freely.

September 3

Dog

Lord, help me to be the person my dog thinks I am.

Unknown

If we could be the people our dogs look up to, then we would be something or somebody. They look to us for their every need. They can't get their own food or water. They depend totally and completely on us. They adore us.

This is how we should be with our Lord. We should look up to Him for our every need. Do we adore Him? He adores us.

September 4

Graduation

Every time you graduate from the school of experience, some one thinks up a graduate program!

Unknown

Oh, how true this is! Just when you think you have things figured out, then the rug is pulled out from under you.

I read everything I could get my hands on about eating disorders when our oldest daughter was diagnosed with anorexia. You can be considered an expert if you read five books in three years on one subject. I needed to know what we were up against. It's extremely important to educate yourself.

The same is true in life. You learn from experience and you figure out what works best for you. God is what's best for you. You get on your knees and cry out to your Father. There's no one more qualified to help you. He knows all.

I had to move to Starkville to get our daughters away from some bad influence and provide for them a safe haven. It was a scary time, but I had to learn to trust God with everything.

To make matters worse, my memory about childhood abuse came back to me. I knew something was wrong because I was having nightmares. It all came flooding back to me in vivid color. I was suddenly transported back to an abandoned house on our property. Needless to say, I became physically sick. God has provided me with some awesome counselors. He can heal all pain and damage from abuse. I'm living proof!

September 5

Rainbow

I do set my bow in the clouds, and it shall be for a token of a covenant between me and the earth.

Genesis 9:13

Today the rainbow is used for all kinds of things, some not good. God gave us the rainbow as a sign never to flood the earth again. We as Christians need to stand up and defend the rainbow. How do you think it makes God feel when He sees it being used for something else? When God gives a special meaning to something, we don't need to mess with it. God might decide to punish those who misuse it.

September 6

Prayer

Don't pray for an easier life; pray to be a stronger person.
Unknown

We've all prayed for an easier life, at some point, I am sure. That's not how it works. God wants us to come to Him for everything we need.

Life's experiences will teach you plenty. How well you learn life's lessons will depend on how strong a person you have become. God promises not to give us more than what the Holy Spirit can handle. When we had to hospitalize our daughter, I had to beg God for strength. When I was told I would lose my eye, I had to beg God for strength. When my husband and I were in marriage counseling, I begged God for strength. When I was told I had macular degeneration disease, I had to beg God for strength. I have degenerative disk disease and I have to beg God for strength every day. Has He ever failed to give me strength? No! Every time I've asked, God has come through for me. Today, I'm a much stronger person and God gets all the credit.

September 7

Idols

Where you go here after depends on what you go after here.
Unknown

    This is kind of a tongue twister, but look closely at its meaning. If you are chasing after money, drugs, women/men, and alcohol; then I suggest a major change. God can take away whatever additions you may have. If you are addicted, then you are playing with Satan. You can't serve two masters. The Bible says, you'll love one and hate the other. I know plenty of people who are fooling themselves into thinking they are saved; but they have evil in their hearts. God can not live in a heart where there is evil. Do a heart check! Your life depends on it!

September 8

Pilot

No wind is favorable for the sailor who doesn't know which direction he is going. Let God be your pilot.

unknown

I write this on placemats and hope it lands in front of the wanderer. So many people are drifting through life. An unmanned boat is of no use to anyone. Let God be your pilot. He knows where you need to go. He knows the way. Follow Him.

September 9

Faith

Faith is telling a mountain to move and being shocked only if it doesn't.
Unknown

Here's another saying I use on placemats at Emmaus. Oh, ye of little faith. Just think what all you could do for God if you had more faith. You can't go out and buy it. Ask God to help you develop more faith. Remember the song, "You've got to have faith, faith, faith?" It takes a lot of faith to make it in this world. I want you to figure out how to grow more faith.

September 10

Number

Teach us to number our days, that we may present to thee a heart of wisdom.

Psalm 90:12

It is a wise man who knows and understands that we won't live forever. Some day will be our last. Act accordingly. Use your time wisely, working for our Lord. Think of the other person. It could be their last day and you're the last person to say a word to them.

When we hear that someone has died, we automatically think back and try to remember our last words with them. Sometimes it works and sometimes it doesn't. I remember telling both my parents that I loved them. They knew that already, but I felt like I needed to say it again.

I've already planned out my funeral and left a letter in my Bible for my girls. The preacher laughed when I gave him a copy, but I wasn't going to leave the details to my husband. He probably doesn't even know my favorite Bible verse.

I don't know about you, but I'm ready for the rapture. My daughter wanted to know if she will be scared because she is afraid of heights. I told her to keep her eyes on Jesus and don't look down.

If there's anything you need to take care of, do it now. Today could be your last.

September 11

Death

And he said, "Behold now, I am old, I know not the day of my death
Genesis 27:2

None of us came with instructions that said how long we would live. If we knew the day of our death, then we would probably live like we wanted up to the last day. God wants us to live for Him and do His work until it's our time to check out. It's important to be ready. Are you ready?

What would you do differently if you knew Jesus was coming today?

September 12

Health

Say to him: "Long life to you! Good health to you and your household! And good health to all that is yours!"

1 Samuel 25:6

Wishing everyone good health is great, even though, we know everyone gets sick from time to time. It's just not possible to live in this world without some sickness. Germs are everywhere.

We can try to do our best by eating healthy, keeping our hands washed, and etc. I'm sure you've heard cleanliness is next to Godliness. I first saw this saying in the teacher's lounge at my first job. Nice try by the secretary.

We need to practice saying this verse to others. May God bless you with good health!

September 13

Character

A mirror reflects a man's face, but what he is really like is shown by the kind of friends he chooses.

Proverbs 27:19

How is your reflection? I've heard of some that refuse to even hang a mirror on the wall in their home. What does this tell you? It tells me, they don't like what they see.

Mirrors reflect whatever stands in front of it. Have you ever had to change friends because you didn't want people to think you were just like them? I know I have. Similar people flock together. Choose your friends wisely.

September 14

The World

For godly sorrow worketh repentance to salvation not to be repented of: but the sorrow of the world worketh death.

2 Corinthians 7:10

You have to be truly sincere when asking God for forgiveness or it doesn't work. God knows your heart so don't try to pull the wool over His eyes like you try on ordinary people. God knows everything.

There will be people who will cry out to God, but God won't hear them because of their hearts. Unbelievers aren't forgiven until or unless they come to Christ. They are a hopeless people doomed to death. That's so sad because they can have salvation. Instead, they have rejected Jesus Christ. They will get what they deserve.

September 15

Charity

And now abideth faith, hope, charity, these three; but the greatest of these is charity.

1 Corinthians 13:13

Charity is love. If you care enough to help another, that is love. Agape is God's love.

Why do you think love is the most important thing we can do for others? There are millions of people who think no one loves them. So what is the greatest gift you can give them? Love. That can be demonstrated in many ways. A smile, a hug, a note, a visit, a ride, and so forth. I always ask if I can give them a hug, first. Some people don't like to be touched because of abuse, so you may have to start with a smile. They have to know they can trust you, first. Don't get behind them. Stay in front, so they can see you at all times. This is extremely important with abused people and vets. Keep your voice at a normal level and keep visits short up front.

If we can show others the love of Christ, it paves the way for the world. Some people have a closed or harden heart and it will take some time and patience to get them to open up. The Holy Spirit will help you know what to do. He knows the heart of the person you are witnessing to on His behalf.

September 16

The Word

In the beginning was the word, and the word was with God, and the word was God.

John 1:1

If you substitute Jesus for word in the verse above, it will put things in a better understanding for you. Jesus was with God from the beginning. Jesus is the Son of God and He was sent to earth as a baby. His parents were Mary and Joseph in name only. Jesus is God's word made flesh. Jesus spoke God's word to all that would listen. Unfortunately, most did not believe Jesus. Have you ever told the truth and people didn't believe you? It's not a good feeling. I'm sure Jesus wasn't happy about their rejection of Him. Nobody likes to be rejected. They called Him a liar. Jesus never sinned so they were accusing an innocent man of a crime. We have people today who sit in our prisons that have been falsely accused. I can only imagine how terrible they must feel. They told the truth, but it didn't matter to the judge or jury. Hopefully, God will find a way for these innocent people to be freed.

I would have loved to live in Jesus' day. To hear Him speak, walk with Him, and eat with Him would have been an honor. I would have liked to wash His feet. I don't think I would have been able to watch Him die. That would have broken my heart into. I'm so thankful, He loved me enough to die for my sins!

September 17

Flesh

And the word was made flesh, and dwelt among us, (and we beheld His glory, the glory as of the begotten of the Father,) full of grace and truth.

John 1:14

What is grace? Grace is what we don't deserve. It's a free gift given by God to us. Grace is undeserved, unconditional, unsought love of God.

A lot of people confuse mercy with grace. Here's the difference. Mercy runs to forgive the prodigal son, while grace slays the lamb to celebrate his return. Mercy is God withholding from us what we deserve and grace gives us what we don't deserve. God wants to give you life and take you to heaven, no matter what you've done in the past. He loves you so! God sought out you. He called you unto Him. If you're reading this book, He is calling you to Him. He's got a crush on you and wants to know you better. I pray you are not giving Him a cold shoulder. Dive into God's word and soak up the love He has for you. God is love!

September 18

Truth

For the law was given by Moses, but grace and truth came by Jesus Christ.

John 1:17

Moses went up on the mountain to have a very private conversation with God. Moses stood in God's presence and it showed when he returned. Moses' hair was now white. Try to imagine what must have taken place on top of that mountain. God wrote the Ten Commandments on stone tablets.

Unfortunately, while Moses was away, the people became restless and decided to have a party. Things got out of control and they decided to build a golden calf. When Moses returned, he became so angry, he threw down the tablets; breaking them into many pieces. So Moses presented the law.

Jesus Christ came much later and brought grace and truth. Do we deserve to have our sins forgiven? I think you know the answer to that. Jesus came to save us from our sins, becoming our grace. We deserve mercy, but got grace, instead. We were taught the truth. Jesus said over and over, "I am the truth."

September 19

Live

Dance like no one is watching.
Sing like no one is listening.
Love like you have never been hurt before.
Live like each day is your last.

Unknown

I love this poem. A friend who has suffered most of her life because of abuse sent it the first time I read it, to me. She only trusts a hand full of people. The abuse has taken over her life and she knows who can heal the damage. It's a matter of letting go and letting God have total control. When you are abused as a child, you have no control over the situation; so when you grow up, you no longer let anyone have total control over you ever again. I've been there and done that.

God instructed me to forgive those who have harmed me, so now I live free. Jesus is the only one who can heal that kind of pain. Give it to Jesus and get involved in charity. It'll take the focus off of you and put it on others. Pass it on!

Be careful with the time. Treat each day like it was your last. Some would take that as, let's party. Remember the prodigal son was a party animal and see where it got him. God warns us to remain sober. You can give praise every day that we are another day closer to meeting our Maker. Amen!

September 20

Grace

For all have sinned, and come short of the glory of God: Being justified freely by His grace through the redemption that is in Christ Jesus:
Romans 3:23-24

There's one thing in this world that is absolute and that's grace. It's offered to all. We've all fallen short and none of us deserve grace, but it's free for the asking. Thank God. If it weren't for grace, we wouldn't be going to paradise. You have to be made righteous to enter the gates of heaven. If your sins haven't been forgiven through Jesus Christ, you will be going to the other place. You have to accept Jesus Christ as your Lord and Savior. He was the sacrifice that died for your sins. Acknowledge that Jesus is the Son of God and that He came to save us. Next, confess your sins and ask God to forgive you. Once this has happened, salvation is secure. When witnessing to others, use these steps. Live your life so others will see Christ through you. Always give the glory and praise to our Lord. Thank God today for saving grace.

September 21

Be Still

And He arose, and rebuked the wind, and said unto the sea, "Please, be still." And the wind ceased, and there was a great calm.

Mark 4:39

Jesus was asleep and the apostles feared for their lives. They woke Jesus saying they feared they were going down. Jesus got up and stood at the end of the boat, raising his arms and speaking to the wind. This was one more time Jesus demonstrated His power to the apostles. They still didn't realize who He was. How did they think He was able to stop the wind, if He was an ordinary man? Jesus was not a man, but God. Were they not told that He was born to a virgin?

Some people thought Jesus was crazy when He claimed to be the Son of God. They were looking for a Messiah and they were sure it wasn't Him. They missed it. The coming of Christ was told hundreds of years before and when He stood before them, they didn't believe. Why do you think they couldn't believe He was the Messiah? Was it because they knew His parents? Whatever the reason, they were so wrong. All that reject Him will have to stand before the throne of judgment and admit that He is Lord. They will have to bow down before Him. They will spend eternity regretting that they had not accepted Him, when they had the chance.

September 22

Grace

God added grace and subtracted sin. He multiplied forgiveness, therefore, keeping division from my life.

Unknown

I read this saying somewhere and wrote it in my notes because I thought it said it all! Thank God for grace! Without grace, we would receive exactly what we deserve which would be death. Instead, God covered us with grace and forgave us of our sins. He didn't have to do that for us, but He loves us so much, that He wanted to. I'm so thankful God has forgiven me. We should be shouting thanks to the rooftops. We could never repay Him for what He has done for us or has yet to do.

Be thankful that He has kept Satan at bay. I wouldn't want what happened to Job, happen to me. Please, Lord, keep Satan away from me. Please protect me from all evil. Thank you, Lord, for your protection today and tomorrow and for all time.

September 23

Blind

I the Lord have called thee in righteousness, and will hold thine hand, and will keep thee, and give thee for a covenant of the people, for a light of the Gentiles; To open the blind eyes, to bring out the prisoners from the prisons, and them that sit in darkness out of the prison house.
Isaiah 42:6-7

What do you think it means for the Lord to keep you? I get a very warm fuzzy feeling when I think of Him holding me. When He held me in ICU, it was out-of-this-world and I was in bad shape. He'll hold you whenever you need Him to. You don't have to be in bad shape.

What is a covenant? It's a promise between you and God. God sent His Son, Jesus, to bring us light and liberty.

Jesus opened the eyes of the blind and healed the sick. He freed people from bondage and He brought light to the world. What do you need today?

September 24

Christianity

First, I thank my God through Jesus Christ for you all, that your faith is spoken of through the whole world.

Romans 1:8

Paul played a huge role in the spread of Christianity through out the world. By 325AD, Christianity had become the dominant religion. One-third of the world's population was now Christian. Paul is thanking God for allowing him to be a part of the way. Later the movement was named Christianity.

You'll notice that all the apostles have become so famous, that schools, hospitals, and important government buildings are named after them. They lived up to their names. They were ordinary men called to greatness. I'm thankful they were so dedicated to our Lord Jesus Christ.

Now Christianity is spreading below the equator into South America and Africa. Millions of lost souls will now hear the "good news". The Great Commission is well on its way to completion. More and more people are going on mission trips. See if there's a mission team near you that you can join or help with finances. Be a part of the Great Commission.

September 25

Trouble

Hear my prayer, O Lord, and let my cry come unto thee. Hide not thy face from me in the day when I am in trouble; incline thine ear unto me: in the day when I call answer me speedily.

Psalm 102:1-2

If you belong to Christ, you have the most divine, most faithful Father that you can call on for help. There is none greater for you to depend on. Take Him with you wherever you go in life.

Seek His face and everything else will fall into place.

September 26

By You

The Lord is with you when you are with Him. If you seek Him, He will be found by you, but if you forsake Him, He will forsake you.
2 Chronicles 15:2

Where is the Lord? Is He with you? I pray you are seeking Him and long for Him to be by your side in all things. I wouldn't dream of going anywhere without Him.

When our daughter, Tiffany drove back and forth to ECS in Cordova, TN, I prayed her all the way to school and back. Driving in Memphis, TN at age 15 is a major task. It's hard for an adult. I drove her for a while and she rode with a friend for a while, but the time came to where she had to go alone. It was one of the hardest things I've had to do. I placed her in God's hands and commanded angels to surround her. It was a long three years, but it was worth the Christian education.

Seek His presence and He'll be there for you. Take Him with you to work today. You'll enjoy His company.

September 27

The Poor

He who gives to the poor will lack nothing, but He who closes his eyes to them, receive many curses.

Proverbs 28:27

This is so true. I have always given to the poor and I have never lacked for anything. My mother taught me to care for the needy, poor, and widows. God requires it of Christians. I have a special passion for children that's why I graduated in elementary education. It breaks my heart to see a child in need.

You can sponsor an orphan here at home or in Africa through www.rafiki-foundation.org. You can even pick which country in Africa you would like. I chose Ghana because we have friends there that we are working with to build churches. If you want information on how to build a church in Russia or Ghana, you can contact John Garrott at P.O. Box 646, Senatobia, MS 38668, or email jgarrott4@aol.com. The website is www.4Mfd.org. We could use your help. God will love you for it. Be the hands and feet of Christ to the world.

September 28

The Bible

When all else fails, read the instructions.

Unknown

    If you don't know already, you'll know before you finish this book that the Bible is full of all kinds of instructions for life. What amazes me is that all the messages are still relevant for life today. God made sure that we would be equipped with exactly what we would need.

    How did God know what we would need today? God knows from the beginning to the end. That's hard for us to understand, but God already knows everything that will happen. He knows what choices you will make before you do. He knows your every thought. You have an all-powerful Father that can do all. That alone should make you feel secure. So next time you need instruction on what you should do, read the Bible.

September 29

Praise

Let everything that has breath, praise the Lord.
Psalm 150:6(NIV)

We have so much to be thankful for, but yet we don't praise the Lord like we should. Why do we find it so hard to do? It should be easy. From the moment we wake up, we should praise His name. Give thanks for the breath that we breathe and the sunrise that welcomes us into the day. Give thanks for your home and the food that sustains you. Give thanks for your family and your friends. Give thanks for your health.

I love to start my day with thanks for being one day closer to heaven. Another day closer to meeting Jesus face to face. Another day closer to being reunited with loved ones. It's been forty-three years since I saw my mother last. The thought of spending eternity with my Lord and my loved ones gives me plenty of reason to get out of the bed and let my heart sing. Praise be to God! Amen!

September 30

Name

Thine eyes did see my substance, yet being unperfected; and in the book all my members were written, which in continuance were fashioned, when as yet there was none of them.

Psalm 139:16

When we accept Jesus Christ as our Lord and Savior, our name is written in the book of life. No one can erase your name. Isn't it awesome that God knows your name? The Master of the universe, the King of Kings, the Lord of Lords, knows your name! Not only does He know your name but also He cares for you.

People love to drop names of important people that they know, but how often do we drop Jesus' name? I use His name every chance I get. If I had my way, I would want everyone to be saved. Jesus wants the same, but we were given free will. Free will to choose or not to choose the Father, which is in heaven.

If you haven't made your choice, I suggest you do so today while you still have a choice.

October 1

Numbers

But the very hairs of your head are all numbered.
Matthew 10:30

The fact that God is keeping up with the numbers of hairs I have on my head is amazing, since I'm losing them very rapidly. That number is spiraling out of control. If I keep losing mine at this rate, I'll need a wig soon.

Why do you think God wanted us to know that He is keeping up with the number of hairs we possess? It tells me that He cares greatly for me. If He knows the number of hairs, then He knows everything about me. He's keeping close tabs on me. He watches over me every minute of the day and night. That's comforting. In this busy world, no one else keeps up with you like that. No one cares enough to know you that well. Relish in the fact that God loves you more than you'll ever know.

October 2

Called

God doesn't call the qualified. He qualifies the called.

unknown

When it was first mentioned to me to write my first book, I knew I didn't have the skills to pull that off. I wasn't even willing to go there, but Dr. Tom Elkin asked me to pray about it. I agreed to pray for 30 days. I knew if it was God's will that He would be able to convince me within that time frame. I remember telling God that I failed freshman English at Miss. State, like He had forgotten. God doesn't forget things like that, like we do. After 30 days, I asked God for a sign just to make sure I was following His will. I turned around and there at eye-level was a sign that I had made for an Emmaus Walk. It's at the top of this page. At that moment, I knew what He wanted me to do. I sat down at the computer with no notes and asked God to speak through me and let me know what to tell. The rest is history.

You are now reading my third adult book. Are you wrestling with something you know God wants you to do?

October 3

Thy Word

Thy word have I hid in mine heart, that I might not sin against thee.
Psalm 119:11

This is exactly why we need to memorize scriptures, so when we're out in the real world, we can recall God's word and it'll guide us through the temptation and still remain pure. Being tempted is not a sin; it's the acting on it. We're tempted every day. Satan is hoping we'll stumble and fall. He's counting on it. Are you going to play into his hands or are you going to use God's word as a shield? Arm yourself with His word before you even consider heading for the door. Remember sin starts with a thought followed by action. Learn to control your thoughts. Sometimes it means changing friends, limiting where you go, changing television channels, or changing your music. God loves an obedient child, just like you.

October 4

Healed

The centurion answered, " Lord, I am not worthy to have you come under my roof; but only speak the word, and my servant will be healed.
Matthew 8:8

I'm assuming the centurion was not saved, but he had heard how Jesus healed the sick and sent for Him. The centurion knew He was not worthy, just like the rest of us. We were made worthy through the cross.

It wasn't until the 4th century that Roman Emperors were lead to Christ. Peter and Paul were responsible for the conversions in Rome. The first time Peter spoke after Christ's death, three thousand people were saved.

Jesus was known by His words of peace and for His miracles. He was the perfect example of forgiveness. His last words were for God to please forgive them for they knew not what they had done. I have prayed the same prayer for those who have attacked me and called me names. Do you need to pray this prayer, also? Learn to forgive so that God will forgive you.

October 5

Remember

I will remember the deeds of the Lord; yes I will remember your miracles of long ago.

Psalm 77:11(NIV)

Why do we need to remember the Lord's miracles, especially since they happened ages ago? Jesus is the same today, tomorrow, and forever. He has not changed, except for His location. He can perform the same miracles today. All he has to do is speak and it will be done. He doesn't have to be here in person. He left the Holy Spirit in His place. The Holy Spirit can do all that Jesus did in the flesh. All you have to do is believe. Is the Holy Spirit living silently within you, waiting on you to call upon it? What are you waiting for?

October 6

The Heart

...For the Lord seeth not as man seeth; for man looketh on the outward appearance, but the Lord looketh on the heart.
1 Samuel 16:7

How many times have we judged a person by how they were dressed? Too many to count, I'm sure. God doesn't care what type clothing we wear, unless it's too seductive for someone's eyes and causes them to sin. We need to double check before we leave the house and see if we are covered appropriately.

What concerns me is the heart. The heart controls our actions and emotions. It's good versus evil. You either have a good heart or you don't. I would rather have a good heart over a high IQ any day. A good heart will serve you well in life. Ask God to give you a good clean heart, if you don't already have one. Only God can change a heart. Remember God is the Master of makeovers. We all need improvement. What would you like for God to change for you?

October 7

Called

The Lord says, "Do not fear, for I have redeemed you; I have called you by name, you are mine."

Isaiah 43:1

Unfortunately, we spend way too much time living in fear. It is a human trait. God is asking us not to be a part of fear because He has paid a very dear price for our sins and we are redeemed! Once the salvation is set in stone, there is nothing we should fear. Even if someone takes our life away here, we are assured of everlasting life in the next world. God is not going to let someone take you out early. God has your date in His hands. We belong to God and everything you see is your inheritance.

You are a child of God. Start acting like it.

October 8

Burden

Are you wrinkled with burdens? Go to church for a face-lift.

Unknown

I think this was one of the church signs that I used at Emmaus. I used it on placemats with a picture of a very wrinkled dog. People are constantly searching for the newest technique for making us look younger than we really are. We are obsessed with our outward appearances when we should be concerned about the inside.

I use to be a vain person, always checking myself in the mirror or my reflection in glass. Now, it's kind of senseless. I wear an eye patch to cover my disfigured eye. I had a tumor removed from behind my left eye, but two years ago I had to have the dying eye removed. The eyelid no longer works, so I just cover it up. You wouldn't believe the comments I get from people. People really need to think before they speak. For some reason, they think it's a joke. Trust me, it's no joke to lose an eye. Even though, I can no longer work, God is using me to further His kingdom.

Present yourself to God. Give Him all your burdens and see what He can do with your life. Don't be amazed! If He can turn me into a writer, just think what He might do with you.

October 9

Witness

Ye are my witnesses, saith the Lord, and my servants whom I have chosen; that ye may know and believe me, and understand that I am He: Before me there was no God formed, neither shall there be after me.
Isaiah 43:10

This verse proves that God is and was the only God ever. How these other people came up with their own God beats me. Somebody had to make them up and pass them down through the generations. Are they in for a rude awakening or what?

God tells us we are His witnesses and He's counting on us to go out into the world and spread the gospel. He also calls us His servants. We are to do His will and be His hands and feet. If you are not currently working for God, then ask yourself what's stopping you. He expects much from us, just like a Father expects his children to help him. God is no different.

October 10

Harvest

[Jesus] said to His disciples, "The harvest is plentiful but the workers are few. Ask the Lord of the harvest, therefore, to send out workers into His harvest field."

Matthew 9:37-38

We all know how plentiful the harvest is in the world. It's really overwhelming. I had to help my father with our acre garden behind our house. He was a soil conservationist and loved growing plants. I on the other hand, did not appreciate all the work it required. Some times I would hoe too fast and accidentally cut some of the pea vines into. To hide my mistake, I would stick the vine back into the soil. My father would later walk along the rows and find a dead vine. He knew what had happened, but he always asked me, "Did you do that?" There was no denying it. He knew I had been working in the garden. Even though, I might not have been the best worker, my dad had only two of us at the time. We offered our best. God wants us to offer our best and go in His name. We need more workers who are willing to witness to the world. Are you willing to go in His name?

October 11

Commands

I praise you, O Lord; teach me your ways...I take pleasure in your laws; your commands I will not forget.

Psalm 119:12,16

If you stop people on the street and ask them to recite the Ten Commandments, I promise you, they can't recall all of them. They remember only what they want to remember. We use to have a huge copy in our study hall at school, but now schools don't display the commandments anymore. Even courthouses have removed God's laws from their grounds. Where will this stop? People are even wanting to remove, "In God we trust," from our money and stop the pledge of allegiance from being said in schools.

I will not forget God's laws no matter what the world does. Write them in your heart.

October 12

The Mouth

Out of the overflow of the heart, the mouth speaks.
Matthew 12:34(NIV)

No one can control your mouth but you. Whatever the heart feels, so speaks the mouth. How quickly it happens. If you don't guard your mouth, you'll be asking people to forgive you later. This is becoming a huge problem with the world. Just watch the news or read the papers and you'll see what I'm talking about. A man killed another man today because he wouldn't give him a cigarette. What has the world come to?

Guard your heart, so your tongue won't feel the need to run off. I have a friend who keeps peppermint in her pocket and when she feels the need to speak and she knows she should keep her mouth shut, she pops a peppermint in her mouth. She needs to do a commercial for the candy company.

October 13

Faithfulness

The psalmist wrote, "I do not hide your righteousness in my heart; I speak of your faithfulness and salvation. I do not conceal your love and your truth."

Psalm 40:10 (NIV)

A true Christian who loves the Lord with their whole heart does not hide anything in their heart. A true Christian talks about God's faithfulness and His grace. A true Christian wants to share the truth and God's love with others. We need to share with others what God has done for us. After all He has done for us, this is the least we can do for Him. If you are a shy person, ask God to give you boldness. Don't hold back your witness for fear what others will say. After all you know the truth and they don't. If they don't accept the truth, it's not your fault. Go in faith.

October 14

Treasure

We have this treasure in clay jars, so that it may be made clear that this extraordinary power belongs to God and does not come from us.
2 Corinthians 4:7(NRSV)

God is the potter and we are the clay. God is to mold us as to how He needs us to be. We are not our own to do as we wish. We were created for a reason. You have to have a teachable heart to conform to God's will. Come to Him and surrender your all to become the person God created you to be. Don't let the world have any part of you. If you do, you won't like what you see.

Remember the one within you is greater than He that is in the world.

October 15

God

O Lord, God of our fathers, are you not the God who is in heaven?
2 Chronicles 20:6(NIV)

There are over 3,000 different Gods, but my God is the only true one. There were none before Him and none will exist after Him. God is the almighty Lord of all. He is the Creator, Healer, Father, and everything else in between. God is all!

What do you need right now for God to do? Bow down before Him and beg Him to help you. He may be waiting for you to ask for help. Ask now. Help is just a prayer away.

God loves you dearly. He would do anything just for you. You are a child of God. He's waiting for you to come to Him. Run unto Him today.

October 16

Genuineness

In this you rejoice, even if now for a little while you have to suffer various trials, so that the genuineness of your faith...may be found to result in praise and glory and honor when Jesus Christ is revealed.
1 Peter 1:6-7 (NRSV)

We've all had trials to test our faith. It's what you do or how you react to trouble that tells if you learned from the experience. Did you trust God to bring you through it or did you come unglued? God wants us to turn to Him. He will give you the strength that's needed to come out the other side of your storm. You have to learn to trust God. Trust is not bought. It's earned over time. Give God praise even in time of trouble. He's there with you. Ask Him to make himself known to you. You'll be surprised what He does for you. Christians have hope when we face tribulations, not so for others.

October 17

Stewards

The Lord God took the man and put him in the Garden of Eden to till it and keep it.

Genesis 2:15 (NRSV)

God created Adam and left the garden in his care. Adam named all the animals and took care of all the plants. Adam lived in a perfect place, but not for long. Their greed for all knowledge got them kicked out of paradise forever.

We as Christians are also expected to take care of what we've been given. Too many people are destroying our parks, beaches, rivers, and seas. If we don't appreciate what God has done for us, He'll take those things away. We are to be stewards of this earth after all it's our inheritance.

Whenever, Jesus wanted to be alone, He always went to a garden to talk to God. Where do you go?

October 18

Silence

For God alone my soul waits in silence.
Psalm 62:1 (NRSV)

It's extremely important to have a quiet time in such a busy world. What ever you have to do to find a quiet spot in your home or backyard, do it for you and God. Next, it's necessary to learn to be a good listener. If you do all the talking, then how are you going to know what God wants to tell you? I love my quiet time. God speaks to us in a still small quiet voice and we have to be listening in order to hear Him. Turn off the television and radio, so there'll be no distractions. Give God your undivided attention. You'll be surprised at what God has to say to you. Happy listening!

October 19

Rescue

Defend the cause of the weak and fatherless; maintain the rights of the poor and oppressed. Rescue the weak and needy; deliver them from the land of the wicked.

Psalm 82:3-4

Our Sunday school class is helping a ministry to unwed mothers called Sav-a-life. We are investing in the life of the mother so she will be better equipped to make better choices in the future for herself and her baby. Hopefully, the mothers will see Christ through us and will want to grow into a beautiful Christian mother. By giving of ourselves, maybe we'll be able to convince the mother that Christ will take care of her, not the world.

I'm so thankful a Christian mother in a Christian home reared me. Was it perfect? Not by any means, but we were taught who was the most important person in our lives. God. The world revolves around Him and Him alone. God has to be number one in your life or you'll find yourself trying to figure out what's wrong. Get your priorities right.

October 20

Faith

Thomas answered him, "My Lord and my God!" Jesus said to him, "Have you believed because you have seen me? Blessed are those who have not seen and yet have come to believe."

John 20:28-29(NRSV)

Thomas was an apostle who needed to see and touch things in order to believe. He's not alone. There are millions of people who feel the same way. Well, Jesus lived over 2,000 years ago. We couldn't all be born in Jesus' day. I haven't seen or touched God, but I believe He exists. Those that walked with Jesus were blessed to have been in His presence. We can only rely on the stories in the Bible as truth. The Bible is books of faith not history. You either believe the whole Bible or not at all. Don't be a doubting Thomas! Believe God is Lord of all!

October 21

Encourage

Encourage one another and build each other up.
1 Thessalonians 5:11(NIV)

We have encouragement cards in the pews at our church. The cards are worth their weight in gold for the love and support they bring to people. I have received many over the years and they seem to arrive at just the right moment.

Just about every Emmaus Walk I've worked, there have been preachers who have come with a heavy load and worn out. Because of all the love and encouragement, the preachers leave on Sunday with their fires rekindled.

The world is hard on all of us, so we need to build each other up. Satan tears down and Christ builds up. Remember that before you speak from here on. Represent Christ and build others up with love, support, and encouragement.

October 22

Orphans

Jesus said, "I will not leave you as orphans; I will come to you."
John 14:18 (NIV)

Ever since my parents died, I have felt like an orphan. I lost my mother when I was 16 years old and two years later I was off to college. I received $88 a month from Social Security and no financial support from my father. I had to learn to support myself by working at the library. I applied for a student loan, but I was told my father made too much money. My grandparents had to pay for two years of tuition or I was going to have to drop out and work for a while. I'm very thankful for their help.

During my college years, I felt very alone, but there was one who had not abandoned me and His name was Jesus. If your parents are gone and you don't feel like you have anyone to turn to; Jesus will be there for you. He promises to provide all your needs.

October 23

Enriched

A generous person will be enriched.
                              Proverbs 11:25 (NRSV)

In the Bible, it says if we have two coats, to keep one and give the other one away. I go through my clothes on a regular basis, but I tend to hold on to things even when I haven't worn them in years, especially if it cost me a good bit of money. I need to do better. We all need to do better when it comes to helping others.

God loves it when we share with others. Life is really hard for most of us. Right now people are suffering from all the high gas prices. Companies are laying off thousands of people. Food prices are climbing higher. Where will it stop?

The churches will have to step up to the plate and help these people who have lost jobs. Food pantries will need to be set up and love offerings will need to be taken up. If we all pitch in, we can help those who need it most. Let's show Christ through our actions.

October 24

Lead

From the end of the earth I call to you, when my heart is faint, lead me to the rock that is higher than I.

Psalm 61:2 (NRSV)

    I see a lot of worry in the faces of those I meet. They are carrying a heavy burden with finances, children, relationships, and sickness. It seems like every week, we hear of someone else who has a life threatening disease. I don't know why, but there seems to be a lot of cancer cases here in Senatobia and even in our church. I'm praying for a cure. We may not live long enough to see it, but maybe some day there will be some medical help made available.

    When my mother was dying from breast cancer, she had an amazing attitude. How could she stay positive while facing a disease that could take her life? My mother had the "rock" as her Father. Sometimes God heals by taking our loved ones to heaven where there is a total healing from everything. Heaven is our real home. Our goal is to make it to heaven. We can't get there unless we die or rapture.

October 25

Training

Fathers, do not exasperate your children, instead bring them up in the training and instruction of the Lord.
Ephesians 6:4 (NIV)

God warns the fathers to be careful not to bring their children to rage. Fathers are responsible to bring their children up in the church, training them in the ways of the Lord. We all need to be good examples. If a father hollers at his children in rage, then the children change from whom they were created to be. The children will internalize the abuse and some will take it out on others passing it down through out the generations.

Sins of the father are sins that have been passed down. If there are sins that have been past to you, then ask God to stop the curse with you today. God will jump at the chance to help you.

October 26

Grace

The Lord said to Paul, "My grace is sufficient for you, for the power is made perfect in weakness."

2 Corinthians 12:9NRSV)

We don't know what thorn Paul had in his side but whatever it was it didn't stop him from carrying out the work of the Lord. There's a reason why we weren't told what his problem was. Everybody can relate to Paul, no matter what his or her problem is. So whatever hurts you, carry on. Ask God for strength and He will see to it that you can move forward. When we don't have the strength, the Holy Spirit can provide. We are made perfect in His righteousness. Don't listen to what the world tells you. Learn to listen to the Father. He's the only one that matters. When you don't know who you are the world will tell you.

October 27

Command

Jesus said, "My command is this: Love each other as I have loved you."
John 15:12 (NIV)

It's hard to love people who are so critical and always finding fault with you. The world is eager to tell you what's wrong with you. This is when you have to call on the Holy Spirit and constantly remind yourself, you are a child of God. If others are judging you, then they are in the wrong. Carry on in the Holy Spirit and keep working for the Lord until He returns.

My siblings tried to silence me when I wrote my first book about my abuse. I made the decision to help other women get on with their lives after abuse. My siblings were wrong in calling me a liar. I was an innocent child and they have turned against me. I turned them over to God to deal with it. I am a child of God, so they are actually attacking God. He will fight my battles for me. In the meantime, I've gone on to write my second book to help those who have lost everything like Job. If I had stopped writing like my siblings wanted I would not have continued doing what God has called me to do. Sometimes, you have to make decisions, but never let people trump God. God will love you for sticking up to them. His will comes first!

October 28

Strength

You, O Lord be not far off; O my strength, come quickly to help me.
Psalm 22:19

It seems like everywhere we turn, we need help from above. As the world grows worse, we will need more and more help. I pray the Lord will come and get us soon and very soon. It's depressing just to watch the news or read the newspapers.

I have a friend who has been suffering over the fact that she did not check on her grandson while he was bushhogging their property. Drew hit a hole and was thrown off the tractor and the bushhog ran over him. We don't know how long he laid there. A garbage truck was driving down the road and saw the tractor going around in circles. Thank goodness help was called and Drew was air lifted to The Med in Memphis, TN. Even though, Drew lay there in need, He was not alone. I feel like angels were surrounding him until help came. Drew will need many surgeries, but he's still with us. He'll have to learn how to walk with man-made legs, but he won't be the first.

When you need help, just cry out to our Father and He'll be there for you.

October 29

Love

How precious is your steadfast love, O God!

Psalm 36:7 (NRSV)

My daughter, Tiffany, had a pretty little pink bear with two pockets on his front. When you pulled his arms out of the pockets and stretched them out, the writing on his paws said, "I love you this much!" When I would ask her how much she loved me, she would stretch out her arms and say, "I love you this much!" Well, Jesus loved you enough to stretch out His arms and let them nail Him to the cross because He loved us this much! How much do you love Him?

October 30

Storms

Paul wrote, "Three times I was beaten with rods, once I was stoned, three times I was shipwrecked, I spent a night and day in the open sea."
2 Corinthians 11:25 (NIV)

Poor Paul had it rough. We think we've had it bad, but I don't think we can top this list. I've been through a lot but I've never been stoned or shipwrecked. He was not a lucky fellow. I admire Paul for continuing to spread the gospel. Most people would have thrown in the towel and gone home. Paul gave his life for our Lord. Would we have gone to Rome knowing how the Christians were being treated? I doubt it.

It's not much different today. Our missionaries are having a very hard time preaching in the world. Some have even lost their lives serving our Lord. We have friends that we are praying for right now. I covered my husband and the mission team while they were in Africa. My friend and her daughter just got back from Panama and I covered them with prayer while they were gone. If you are not able to go like me, you can pray for those who are willing and able to go in His name.

October 31

Worry

"Martha, Martha," the Lord answered, "You are worried and upset about many things, but only one thing is needed. Mary has chosen what is better."

Luke 10:41-42NIV)

Martha was probably running around with her head chopped off, barking orders at Mary. Where was Mary? She was sitting at the feet of Jesus, hanging on to every word that He spoke. I know where I would have been. I would have been at Jesus' feet, also. Try to imagine being that close to Him. That had to be awesome! Some day we'll get that opportunity in paradise.

Have you chosen what's better?

November 1

Vision

Paul had a vision. There stood a man of Macedonia pleading with him and saying, "Come over to Macedonia and help us".

Acts 16:9 (NRSV)

How well do we listen? I'm thankful that my husband had come home when I fell in the sunroom. I tripped over a footstool breaking my right arm down the center of the bone and chipping my right shoulder. I was in so much pain, I couldn't get up. As my husband walked by the door on his way back to work, he heard my moaning. He stepped into the room and asked me what was the problem. I told him I thought I had broken my arm. In his haste, he grabbed my left arm and jerked it. I screamed bloody murder! I had to ask him to gently help me up. I felt like the old lady on the commercial who would say, "I've fallen and I can't get up!" I couldn't understand why she couldn't get up, till I found myself in the same situation.

We need to become super sensitive to listening to other's needs when we're in such a hurry. If my husband had rushed out the door, I would have laid there till he came home again. Tune your ears.

November 2

Mistakes

All of us make many mistakes.
James 3:2 (NRSV)

We have all fallen short of the glory of God. I don't want to compare my mistakes to anyone else's. I can look back and see how stupid some of my mistakes were. You have to wonder, "What was I thinking?" It does no good to stew over our mistakes. You need to ask for forgiveness and move on. It's important to learn from our mistakes or we'll repeat them. I certainly don't want to repeat any of mine. How about you?

I feel like it helps reading God's word every day to stay on the narrow path. When you fall, get right back up. As we strive to become more like Christ, your ability to resist temptation, gets stronger with each passing day. Ask God for strength and He'll provide. He wants you to become stronger.

November 3

Help

The angel of the Lord said, "Hagar, servant of Sarai, where have you come from, and where are you going?

Genesis 16:8(NIV)

Angels are around us all the time. They are commanded by God to protect us in our time of need.

When our oldest daughter, Heather, was in a wreck on her way to work, a nurse pulled across her lane. Heather didn't have enough time to do anything, but slam into Mrs. Scott's van. The impact of the accident turned the van over and then it hit the curb, righting it again. Mrs. Scott said that she felt a presence holding her back in her seat and it wasn't the seatbelt. We felt like it was an angel protecting her. Mrs. Scott ended up with a cracked vertebrate, but things could have been much worse. Heather had bruises and abrasions from the seatbelt and the airbag. Many prayers were said over this accident. If you had seen Heather's car, you would have thought the person driving it might not have survived. It was a total loss. I'm sure angels were there for both our daughter and Mrs. Scott that day.

Have you felt angels around you? I have. I've been in eight wrecks.

November 4

Angels

The angel of the Lord encamps around those who fear Him, and delivers them.

Psalm 34:7(NRSV)

Have you ever found yourself in a dangerous situation? Several times I felt an attack coming on and I reacted accordingly. I guess you could say that the Lord warned me of what was fixing to happen.

The first time I was visiting my cousin in Memphis, TN. I had walked from her apartment to a nearby store. As I was waiting for traffic to pass so I could cross the street, I noticed a truck slowing down as it neared me. I saw three men in the truck staring at me. One was opening his door to jump out. The Lord warned me that they were not good men, so I darted across several lanes of traffic. I looked back over my shoulder as I ran to my cousin's apartment. I wanted to know if they were turning around. That was a close call.

My second warning came as I was walking to my husband's truck in Jackson, MS. I had taken my niece and my girls shopping at the mall west of Jackson. I had been told to be careful by a neighbor. I noticed two young men following us. I immediately unlocked the truck, threw my daughter across the seat and told her to unlock the other door. I threw in the shopping bags and reached for a tool in the cabinet behind the cab of the truck. The young men backed off when they noticed how mad I was. Was there an angel there that day? I believe there was. Thank God for angels!

November 5

Persistence

Be persistent in prayer, and keep alert as you pray, giving thanks to God.

Colossians 4:2 (TEV)

Most of my prayers are for thanks. Some spend their time asking for what ever they need, but always give thanks for what you have. If you are not a thankful person, then God might hold back on your blessings.

Maybe it's because I've had so many things to happen to me, but I can remember being thankful as a child. I think it's taught. I can remember my mom telling me to thank someone for her kindness. There was a lady that always sat behind us at church. Every Sunday she would comment on my hair and always had to touch it. I had to be taught to thank her for her comments.

Next time someone gives you a compliment, be sure and thank him or her for their kind words. Next time, you pray, thank God for all that He has done for you and has yet to do. God loves a thankful heart.

November 6

Rest

[Jesus] said to them, "Come away to a deserted place all by yourselves and rest a while." For many were coming and going, and they had no leisure even to eat.

Mark 6:31 (NRSV)

Rest is what the world needs the most. People are rushing here, rushing there, and sometimes meeting themselves in the road. I've been there and done that. When I quit teaching, I threw out the alarm clock.

My husband and I have learned that we need more rest as we age. My husband takes a 30-minute nap after lunch. I've learned to rest mid morning and mid afternoon to relieve my back and legs. If I don't get my rest, I'll need a pain pill when I go to bed.

We have to learn sometimes to say no to all the activities that surrounds us. Learn your limitations.

On Sunday afternoon, we take a nap. I didn't understand why my parents always took a nap, but now I know why. The Sabbath is a day of rest created by God for us.

November 7

Work

To him who by the power of work within us is able to accomplish abundantly far more than all we can ask or imagine, to Him be glory.
Ephesians 3:20-21

I have learned so much by working Emmaus Walks. When I was asked to be on the prayer committee, I felt inadequate and almost turned down the opportunity. My husband and a friend encouraged me to pray about it. I would have missed an amazing opportunity if I had said no. I grew so much in that one weekend.

It was the second time I served on the prayer committee that I actually saw God's hands at work. I was told to go to the men's cabin and pray over a sick young man. I grabbed my anointing oil and headed for the door. I prayed all the way to the cabin, asking God to heal this young man. I went in God's name, but God did all the work. I anointed the young man and said a prayer with him. An hour later, he was in the conference room. I believed God would heal him and he believed that God could. Faith played an important part of the healing. We should never doubt the awesome power of God.

November 8

Adoption

You did not receive a spirit of slavery to fall back into fear, but you have received a spirit of adoption. When we cry, "Abba! Father!" it is that very spirit bearing witness with our spirit that we are children of God.
Romans 8:15-16(NRSV)

So many people have trouble trusting God because they had issues with their earthly fathers. I wasn't real close to my father because he had a temper that sometimes exploded. I never knew if something I said or did would set him off. I learned to keep my distance. I can't stand to be around someone who hollers or even raises his or her voice to this day.

What effected my relationship with men the most was the betrayal by my brother. I learned at an early age that I couldn't trust men. Combine that with a troubled relationship with my dad, and you'll understand why I had trouble trusting God. It took me years to get past the hurt.

God can heal all damage done by others. God wants us to be happy and healthy so why not let Him heal you. He's your loving Father. You are His child.

November 9

Prize

Paul wrote, "I do not claim that I have already succeeded or have already become perfect. I keep striving to win the prize for which Christ Jesus has already won for me to Himself."
Philippians 3:12 (TEV)

Will we ever reach a point where we are perfect? No! As long as there is breath, there will always be room for improvement. We need to strive to be more Christ like each and every day till He returns. Keep your eyes focused on Jesus because He is the prize.

God will forgive you for what you've done wrong. His Son Jesus Christ paid for all your sins past, present, and future. Christ makes us righteous enough to enter the gates of heaven. Amen!

November 10

Come

Jesus said, "I have come in order that you might have life-life in all its fullness."
James 10:10

Remember when Peter saw Jesus walking on the water? Peter was doing fine until he looked down. Down Peter went and Jesus reached out and grabbed him and pulled him back up to safety.

I have fallen so many times and thank goodness the last three times, there was no permanent damage to my knees. I was alone when it happened but Jesus was there to help me up. I have since bought some rubber backed rugs to go in my sunroom. My balance problem is due to having only one eye, so I have to be very careful. I don't let the balance problem keep me home. I don't let the health problems rob me of my fullness of life, either. By keeping my eyes on Jesus, I'm free.

Is there anything keeping you from your fullness of life?

November 11

Scar

No one has greater love than this, to lay down one's life for one's friends.

John 15:13 (NRSV)

Notice it didn't say for a family member, but a friend. To lay down one's life is the ultimate gift. I've never had to donate any body parts or have anyone donate anything for me, but I know people who have had transplants. I've donated blood before and I'm an organ donor. My husband made the remark that by the time I get through with my body, no one will want any of my parts. That's not true. He doesn't know it but I'll donate his parts if he goes before me.

If you're interested in being a living donor, contact The Living Bank in Houston, TX by calling 713-528-2971. You won't need your old body. You'll get a new glorified body in heaven. Amen! Thank Jesus for laying down His life for you!

November 12

Sign

I gave them my Sabbaths, as a sign between me and them, so that they might know that I the Lord sanctify them.
Ezekiel 20:12 (NRSV)

The Sabbath was given to the Israelites as a remembrance to remain holy and give them rest. Without Sunday when would we find time to study His word and fellowship with Him and our brothers and sisters in Christ? We need that bond. We need to rest and know that God is in control. By resting we show God that we trust Him to handle things for us. While we sleep, God is at work. Thank you, God for granting me rest.

November 13

Evil

If God be for us, who can be against us?

Romans 8:31

    I know it seems as if the world is against you. Well, it is. There will be a fight of good against evil, till Jesus returns. That's why I'm hoping for a quick return. It won't be quick enough for me. I'm ready now. Whatever the day and the hour, I'll be ready. Most will not!

    What can we do to help unsaved people become saved? We can become their friend and show them God's love. We can invite them to our church. We can invite their children to Vacation Bible School. We can send them encouragement cards. We can help them with their needs. We can share what Christ has done for us.

    Remember we are not to live in fear, no matter what's going on around us. Walk with confidence, knowing that God walks with you always. Who's got your back?

November 14

Lamp

Thy word is a lamp unto my feet, and a light unto my path.
Psalm 119:105

    I literally need a light for my feet, but this is not what the written message means. If you dive into God's word, you'll get a new perspective on life. You will suddenly start seeing the world differently. Scriptures that you didn't understand before, have new meanings.

    God's word will make the road easier and clearer to follow. When using a flashlight, the light is on where you need to go while the surroundings remain dark. In other words, God's word will help keep you focused on the goal at the end of your pathway of life. Satan will set up roadblocks and hazards, but keep your focus on Jesus. If you fall off the path, get right back on track. There is nothing God can't forgive except not believing in His Son. Jesus is the light of the world. From where does your light come?

November 15

Live

Continue to live in [Christ Jesus], rooted and built up in Him, strengthened in the faith as you were taught and overflowing with thankfulness.

Colossians 2:6-7 (NIV)

One of the happiest days of my life was when my girls walked down the aisle to accept Jesus Christ as their Savior. I was singing in the choir and I started crying and couldn't stop. These were tears of joy. Next came their baptism. Dr. Lloyd baptized them together in the same water, which was very moving for everyone who was there that day. I'm glad my father was able to attend. It was July 10, 1988. Tiffany's birthday was the next day. She was nine years old. Heather was eleven.

Why is July 11th important? That was the date that my mother died in 1965. July was a very depressing month for me until God changed it. God allowed Tiffany to be born on July the 11th, so I wouldn't grieve on that date anymore.

The girls' baptism was the last big event my father would attend. He died July 22, three years later. I'm thankful that my father got to see the girls baptized. I'm thankful my parents are reunited. I'm thankful that some day we'll all be together in paradise. We have a lot of catching up to do and we'll have eternity to do it. Amen!

November 16

Clay

O Lord, you are our Father; we are the clay, and you are our potter; we are all the works of your hand.
Isaiah 64:8(NRSV)

I've never taken pottery classes but I've heard it's not easy. You have to find a center balance to make the clay conform to your hands. We are very much like clay. God is the center balance and with His guidance, He tries to mold us into what He needs us to be. God is the potter and we are the clay.

Unfortunately, a lot of people are not willing to surrender themselves to God. They can't seem to give up all control. The funny thing is they really don't have control over their lives. God has control, whether they realize it or not. They have free choice but that's it. If they don't get right, they will get left behind.

November 17

Miracle

Taking the five loaves and the two fish, [Jesus] looked up to heaven, and blessed and broke the loaves, and gave them to his disciples to set before the people, and He divided the two fish among them all.
                                                            Mark 6:41

    This was one of my favorite stories in the Bible. The apostles were getting worried because they had no way of feeding all the people. They couldn't rush out and buy enough bread and fish to feed 5,000 people. Jesus wasn't worried. He knew what He was going to do. It was a simple boy who came forward and offered his lunch to Jesus. Jesus took the two fish and five loaves of bread and asked God to bless the food. God blessed it all right. There was enough to feed everyone, even with some left over. All these people witnessed a miracle and they didn't leave hungry that day.
    Does Jesus still perform miracles today? You know it!

November 18

Promise

By faith Abraham, even though he was past age...was enabled to become a father because He considered him faithful who had made the promise.

Hebrews 11:11-12 (NIV)

I can only imagine how Abraham felt when God told him a nation would rise up out of his seed. Wonder if Abraham was related to Thomas? Oh, ye of little faith. Sarah over heard what God had in His plans and she laughed. She was well beyond childbearing years, so I kind of understand her disbelief. But when God says something is going to happen, we need to seriously listen. God is not going to tell you a story. When God speaks we need to listen.

Remember when Zechariah was told he would have a son and he laughed. Zechariah couldn't speak till the baby was born. He named his son John the Baptist.

Learn to listen to God. He won't steer you wrong. God wants the best for us. He loves us more than you'll ever know. Just when we think things are beyond help, God comes through.

November 19

Coming

He which testifieth these things saith, "Surely I come quickly." Amen. Even so, come, Lord Jesus. The grace of our Lord Jesus Christ be with you all. Amen.

Revelation 22:20-21

These are the last words in the Bible. I hold these words close to my heart. It's like waiting for Christmas to come. Our precious gift is waiting to come get us. God is the only one who knows the date and hour. Don't listen to those who claim they have figured it out. They can't know. Jesus doesn't even know.

The last sentence wishes you grace from above. Grace is only God given. It's free, just for you.

What can you do for God today?

November 20

Friends

The ornament of a house are the friends who frequent it.
Emerson

How true this quote is! I count my friends when I think of wealth. Friends are God's gift to us.

When my husband and I attended Emmaus, the number of friends multiplied. We've worked walks for twelve years now and we add about eighty new friends every walk we work. There's no other activity that will add friends at this rate. These are prayer warriors that you can call on in a crisis. These are brothers and sisters in Christ. Why wait till heaven to enjoy your friends in Christ?

Tell your friends today how much you appreciate them. They'll love you for it!

November 21

Friend

A true friend reaches for your hand and touches your heart.
unknown

    You have the power to leave heart prints on someone's heart today. Sometimes it is just some kind words, sometimes it's encouraging words, sometimes it's doing a chore for someone, and sometimes it's just a hug. You should know your friends best so pick what you think best suits your friends. It may be as simple as buying lunch or cooking supper for them.

    I have a friend that I like to go eat with about every three months. We'll go get us a really good steak. We don't need a holiday or a reason to celebrate. We just celebrate our friendship.

    One thing you can always do for your friends is to include them in your prayers. We all need prayers!

November 22

Oak

Today's mighty oak is just yesterday's nut that held its ground.
unknown

I love this quote. If we just learn to hold our ground and not cave into temptation, we might become great Christians.

We start out as a tiny acorn and we learn how to build a foundation that will last us a lifetime. The foundation is critical to everything that will follow. When a trial or tribulation hits, it's like a sumani. It'll knock you off your feet before you realize what's going on. Your faith will keep your head above water and will bring you to a safe place where you can rest. You might end up with a few bruises, but you'll have your life. Bruises will go away with time. It's during these trials that you'll realize just who you really are. You'll also realize just how powerful your Father is, also. He's bigger than big. He's huge! God is the ultimate life preserver. He's tough and everlasting and He's yours!

November 23

Sinners

I came not to call the righteous, but sinners to repentance.
                                                      Luke 5:32

Jesus came to save the world. We've all sinned and need redemption. No one is greater than the next person is. God sees us as equals. Our society likes to group people according to their social class, race, and nationalities. God doesn't do that.

When the end comes, it won't matter if you owned a two-story house with a three-car garage. It won't matter how much money you had in the bank. All that will matter is if you are a follower of Christ. Christ died for your sins, so that you will be righteous enough to get through the gates of heaven. Christ will return to collect His own.

Who do you belong to? Are your sins forgiven?

November 24

Gone

Heaven and earth shall pass away, but my words shall not pass away.

Matthew 24:35

Have you ever wondered how the Bible has survived over 2,000 years? It's because God said it would not pass away. God has made sure that the Bible has been past down over the ages. The Bible is the most published book ever. It has remained intact just like God instructed for it to be. The books of the Bible are books of faith not history. Stories that have encouraged millions of people over time.

If you had lived in the Bible days, would your faith and love for Christ been amazing enough to make it into the Bible? I hope so.

November 25

Lord

Not everyone that saith unto me, Lord, Lord, shall enter into the kingdom of heaven; but he that doeth the will of my Father, which is in heaven.

Matthew 7:21

    In my opinion, if you are seeking God's will, then you are sincere in claiming Jesus Christ as your Lord and Savior. I've seen people walk down the aisle because they felt pressured by their parents or other family members. They weren't really seeking Jesus as their Master. They were just walking through the motions. That doesn't count.

    There's a difference in knowing of Jesus and believing in Jesus. Satan knew of Jesus Christ and God because he started out in heaven with both of them. Satan wanted God's job and led a rebellion against Him. Satan was thrown out of heaven with 3,000 angels in tow. Have you noticed that angels don't get a second chance?

    Thank God for sending His Son to save us from the bondage of Satan. Thank God we get another chance.

November 26

Seek

But seek ye first the kingdom of God, and His righteousness; and all things shall be added unto you.

Matthew 6:33

Your salvation is the first thing you need to secure in this world. Once that is complete, you are made righteous enough to enter the next world. We are to live a life that reflects Christ to others. By our actions of love and kindness, we can show the way to those who are lost. When they see how happy you are and how peaceful you live your life, they are going to want what you have. The lost have an empty space inside and are constantly seeking something to fill that void. They will not find anything that will satisfy till they find Christ. Only Christ can satisfy the heart.

If you have friends that you aren't sure if they are saved, they probably aren't. I feel like if they were saved, you would know by their actions and language. Friends don't let friends go to hell. All that's needed are a few simple questions. Do you know where you're going if you were to die right this very minute? Who is Jesus? Why did Jesus come to earth, when He could have stayed in heaven? These questions will get you started.

Have a blessed day!

November 27

Master

No man can serve two masters: for either he will hate the one, and love the other; or else he will hold to the one, and despise the other. Ye can not serve God and mammon.

Matthew 6:24

There are so many people claiming to be a Christian, but they are not in church and they are continuing in their old habits. When a person is saved, all things become new. If you don't see new behavior, then I doubt they seriously turned their life over to Christ. Jesus will accept you where you are, but He doesn't leave you there.

I can't tell you why people say one thing and do another. Maybe it's social pressure from work or the community to present themself as a Christian. Maybe it's to get family members off their back. Every person is held accountable for his or her own salvation. You can't wish someone saved. You can't love God and serve Satan. God can not live in an evil heart. There's room for only one master. Whom will you serve?

November 28

Ways

Thus saith the Lord of hosts; "Consider thy ways".
Haggai 1:7

Everything we do, we're held accountable for our actions. You can't claim the devil made you do it. You have to be a willing participate to sin. If you invite Satan in, it's your fault. You can't blame this on anyone but yourself. Our society loves to blame someone else for how they turned out. That's a copout!

Do a self-evaluation today and see if there is anything you need to get rid of. Do you tell lies? Do you gossip? Do you watch television shows that are a bad influence? Do you use bad language? Do you drink too much?

Consider your ways and choose today to be a better servant of the Lord.

November 29

Joy

The Lord thy God in the midst of thee is mighty; He will save, He will rejoice over thee with joy; He will rest in His love, He will joy over thee with singing.

Zephaniah 3:17

    I'm a curious person by nature. I'm wondering what song my Lord sings over me. I know it's hard to believe that Jesus would be so joyful about us. He wouldn't have said it if it weren't so. I'm just glad that He finds joy in loving me and watching over me.

    I can remember the joy I had as a parent, watching my girls speak their first words, sing their first songs, get their first tooth, and take their first steps. I imagine our Lord feels the same emotions in watching us. Watching us walk down the aisle in His name, being baptized, bringing others to Him, and serving others. I can see my Lord rejoicing because we desire to be obedient for Him.

    I can't wait to look Him in the eyes! I picture myself running to Him and Him swinging me around and off my feet. Oh, what joy that will be! Can you picture Christ Jesus? Can you imagine the joy He has over you?

November 30

Hold

The Lord is good, a strong hold in the day of trouble; and He knoweth them that trust in Him.

Nahum 1:7

If you are in trouble, there's no one stronger to call on. He knows your name despite the number of followers. He knows everything about each and every one of us. He knows your needs even before you speak. We would need a computer to keep up with all the information He knows and then the hard drive still wouldn't be able to handle all of it. Thank goodness, Jesus doesn't need a computer. I'm so thankful, He's so powerful and He doesn't have that holier than thou attitude that most possess when they are rich and famous. He is humble and kind to everyone. He truly cares.

Do you trust Jesus with your life?

December 1

Wise

And they that be wise shall shine as the brightness of the firmament; and they that turn many to righteousness as the stars forever and ever.
Daniel 12:3

    We are not born wise when it comes to religion. You can have a high IQ and be totally lost. We become wise by studying God's word and learning His ways. A foolish man charges forward in life with reckless abandonment. A wise man obeys God's laws. A wise man seeks God's will, not his own.

    A wise man loves the Lord with his whole heart and will want to share the gospel with others. There will be many rewards in heaven for a wise man. The fool will get what he deserves.

    Are you a wise person or a fool?

December 2

Restore

I will seek that which was lost, and bring again that which was driven away, and will bind up that which was broken, and will strengthen that which was sick: But I will destroy the fat and the strong; I will feed them with judgment.

Ezekiel 34:6

These are the words from the judge Himself. Our Lord will heal the sick and restore those who have lost everything. He will bind up things that are broken and make them new again. Jesus will correct whatever has been done wrong to you. There may not be much justice in this world, but the next is nothing but justice. You can count on Jesus to handle all your problems.

Learn to turn your problems over to Jesus and watch Him work. He is so much better at problem solving than we are. Jesus is the Master of everything. He can do so much more than we can. Don't practice revenge. Give it to Jesus, it's better than you going to jail. Trust me on this one.

December 3

I Am

Behold, I am the Lord, the God of all flesh: Is there anything too hard for Me?

Jeremiah 32:27

Let's face facts. There is no one other than God, smarter than God is, more powerful than God is, or more creative than God is. God is the man! Put Him number one in your life and you'll create a center balance that no one can rock. He is the ultimate foundation. There is none better.

We've all bought things that weren't made well and over time they completely fell apart on us. Well, those are earthly items. God is not an earthly creation. He is eternal! God is everlasting.

There is nothing God can not do. There is nothing that can dethrone God or even rock His boat. God is a spirit, but yet He is solid. You can depend on Him in every situation. He covers it all!

December 4

Answer

And it shall come to pass, that before they call, I will answer; and while they are yet speaking, I will hear.

Isaiah 65:24

Sometimes things happen and we say it was a coincidence, but we, as Christians know it was a God thing. Are you going to leave things to chance, or are you going to depend on God? I've never been a lucky person so I'm not going to live on chance. I know from where my strength comes and it's not luck.

Ask people at the casinos if they consider themselves to be lucky people? Most will say they are not lucky, but yet they'll sit there and steadily put money in the machines. Where is the logic? Gone with the wind, I guess.

Remember God always answers our prayers. Sometimes it's, no. Trust Him to know what's best for you. Pray without ceasing.

December 5

Mouth

So shall my word be that goeth forth out of my mouth: It shall not return unto me void, but it shall accomplish that which I please, and it shall prosper in the thing where to I sent it.

Isaiah 55:11

    According to this verse, we are not wasting our breath when we witness to others. You may plant a seed and not see the results, but still the Lord's work was done. Maybe in heaven, we'll get to see the results. Maybe the person that was saved, will look you up and thank you for caring enough to plant that seed.

    When Don Piper was killed in a car wreck, he said that his Sunday school teacher was at the gate. There were also other people who had helped him to become a Christian at the gate to greet him. I will love to see my teachers at the gate when it's my time. Who will you see at the gate?

December 6

Gift

A friend is a gift you give yourself.

R. L. Stevenson

I'm sure you remember the song, "What A Friend We Have In Jesus." There is no greater friend available to you. He loves you unconditionally and will do anything for you. The song talks about all the sins and grief we bear and the peace we give up when we don't come to Jesus. It also asks you if you can find a friend who is so faithful as Jesus. I can tell you right now, no! As much as I love my friends, they are human and will let you down from time to time. That's normal. Jesus will not fail you. Isn't that amazing?

No friend sticks closer than your Father Jesus Christ does. He's your best friend. If you have no other friends, make sure you have Jesus Christ. That's all that matters. You'll have millions of new friends in heaven. Amen!

December 7

Confess

Whosoever therefore shall confess Me before men, him will I confess before My Father, which is in heaven. But whosoever shall deny Me before men, him will I also deny before My Father, which is in heaven.
Matthew 10:32-33

Have you ever denied that you knew someone? We are warned in this verse, that if we deny knowing Christ, He'll deny knowing us. Christians have been mistreated from the beginning of time and things will get worse. Just remember this verse, when you are questioned about being a Christian.

Several years ago at Columbine, the students were asked to stand up if they were a Christian. Some stood up and they were shot dead. If you had been in that library, would you have been able to stand up for Christ? I hope so. Some day it may come to that.

December 8

The Gate

Enter ye in at the strait gate: for wide is the gate, and broad is the way, that leadeth to destruction, and many there be which go in thereat: Because strait is the gate, and narrow is the way, which leadeth unto life, and few there be that find it.

Matthew 7:13-14

    We had a special gate on our farm that would allow a person to pass through from one area to another with out having to unlatch the gate. I called it a pass through. You had to side step to make it through. It was a narrow path.

    When I read this verse, it reminds me of this very narrow gate. So is the gate into heaven. The road to this gate is also narrow. If you have committed your life to Christ and you are obedient to God's laws, then you already know how narrow is the way. There are so few that is willing to follow Christ. I pray you are included in that number. I hope to see you at the gate.

December 9

Hearing

So then faith cometh by hearing, and hearing by the word of God.
Romans 10:17

We first hear about Jesus from our parents, Sunday school teachers, or others. We learn about His miracles, study His life, and read His word. Even the songs we sing teach us a great deal. Now, it's important to take what we've learned and go out into the world and practice what we've learned.

It's been proven that if we don't apply what we've learned within the first 24 hours, we lose 60% of that knowledge. That's why it's so important to read our Bible on a regular basis. We need to surround ourselves in His word. His word becomes our shield.

When you get my age, learn to write scripture and post it where it can be seen and carry it on you. Sometimes, I put it on an index card and place it in my car. Every time I get in the car, I recite the verse. Try it. The going thing now is to put the Bible on your ipod or portable CD or DVD player.

December 10

Love

Owe no man anything, but to love one another: for he that loveth another hath fulfilled the law.

Romans 13:8

Love makes the world go round. I know it makes life easier on you if you learn to love others. Some like to be an island and keep to themselves. I don't see anything wrong with that, but if you work for the Lord; what can you do when you're isolated from the world?

God requires us to love one another. If you don't love others, then how can you tell them about Christ, who is love? We have a jail ministry team at our church. Sometimes, you know who's in jail, but most of the time, they are strangers. I visited a former student once. I saw his name in the paper and made the decision to go visit him. I had not seen him since he finished sixth grade. He was caught selling drugs and by the time I got there, he was very remorseful. He went to prison and should be out by now. I told him to make the most of the time in jail by witnessing to others. I feel like he did. I told him I would be praying for him. He asked me to call his mother when I got home. She thanked me for going to see him.

We need to care enough about others that we are willing to love them through Jesus Christ. Love them first, then share the gospel with them.

December 11

None

As it is written, there is none righteous, no, not one.
Romans 3:10

Most of us know this, but there are a whole lot more that think they are above all others. They are only fooling themselves. We've all fallen short, but those who chose to follow Christ are redeemed. We are never to think we are better than anyone else is.

I had a friend once that said I was going to be rich from writing books. I told her, "No way." I give away more than I sell. I'm not in it for the money. I'm trying to share my wisdom and life experiences with others, so they won't make the same mistakes I've made. I want everyone to love the Lord, like I do. I have all the joy and peace God can give me. If others criticize you, they don't have enough to do. Rise above them.

December 12

Sin

For the wages of sin is death, but the gift of God is eternal life through Jesus Christ our Lord.
Romans 6:23

Before Jesus returns everyone will have had an opportunity to accept Him as Lord. Woe unto those who remain after the rapture. I'm not sure what happens after the saints are gone, but I wouldn't want to be left behind to find out. Some say, that no one will be saved after the rapture. I heard Dr. Adrian Rogers say that if we can't accept Jesus now, why would we accept Him later? I wouldn't run the risk of waiting. You could die in an accident or from a heart attack and there wouldn't be enough time to accept Jesus Christ as your Savior. Tell your family and friends, they need to decide today, whom they will serve. They need their name in the book of life, now. It's free.

December 13

Cross

For the preaching of the cross is to them that perish foolishness: but unto us which are saved it is the power of God.

1 Corinthians 1:18

Those that crucified Jesus on the cross were insane, in my opinion. They knew He performed miracles, but yet they couldn't bring themselves to admit, He's the Son of God. They were fearful of Him. He was growing in popularity and they feared He would control the masses.

We can relate to their fear when we see someone running for president that we know would not make a good leader of our country. If a Christian is not the leader, then God may take His hand of protection off of our country. We surely don't want that to happen. We need all the help we can get. Every time you look at the cross, be reminded of God's awesome power.

December 14

Glory

Whether therefore ye eat, or drink, or whatsoever ye do, to all to the glory of God.

1 Corinthians 10:31

As we draw to the end of the year, let's remember not to over do the eating and drinking that goes along with the holidays. When we abuse these things, we're not glorifying God. People are always watching and it could have an effect on your witness. As Christians we need to be good examples. Our bodies are temples and we need to treat them accordingly. Don't cause someone else to sin because they were copying you.

You can live life to its fullness with out the alcohol and indulgent foods. Get healthy. You'll love yourself for it.

December 15

Eternal

While we look not at the things which are seen, but at the things which are not seen: for the things which are seen are temporal; but the things which are not seen are eternal.

2 Corinthians 4:18

I love to imagine what's there, that we can't see. I like to picture Jesus Christ and God walking with me. I like to picture angles surrounding me. I like to picture myself in heaven with my loved ones. How about you? It's not hard to do. Try it.

Everything we see here will be destroyed at the end. We'll carry nothing from this life with us when we leave, so don't get attached to any earthly possessions.

Your treasures will be in heaven waiting on you.

December 16

Love

Husbands love your wives, even as Christ also loved the church, and gave Himself for it.

Ephesians 5:25

This is God's instruction for our husbands. We are expected to do the same. We all need to love one another as Christ loves us. We fail so miserably at it because we don't understand the scope or magnitude of God's love. When we realize how much He loves us, then it makes it easier for us to love ourselves and then others. You have to love yourself, first. Remember God loved us first before we ever knew Him. He chose us first. That's awesome!

Who loves you? Who do you love?

December 17

Money

For the love of money is the root of all evil: which while some coveted after, they were erred from the faith, and pierced themselves through with many sorrows.

1 Timothy 6:10

    We all know we need money to live, but it is the love of money that will get you into trouble. Most think money will solve their problems, but it will actually bring more problems. Some think money will make them happier. Not so! Happiness comes from within. Only God can satisfy the heart, not money.

    Remember to give God a tenth of your earnings. It's all His and He is only asking for a tenth.

December 18

Commit

And the things that thou hast heard of Me among many witnesses, the same commit thou to faithful men, who shall be able to teach others, also.

2 Timothy 2:2

We are not to keep things of God to ourselves. We are to share what we've learned and set examples for our children and others. We are to inspire others with our charity and love for others.

Our jail ministry touches more than just the prisoners. The team has been blessed as well as the families of the prisoners. We tend to think of prisoners as throwaways. God doesn't see them that way and neither should we think of them that way. They are just as important to God as we are. God loves everyone.

Take God's lead and reach out to those less fortunate.

December 19

Doers

But be ye doers of the word, and not hearers only, deceiving your own selves.

James 1:22

How many times have we sat in church and heard God's word, only to walk out the door and not do anything we heard in the sermon? Too many to count I'm sure. Some daydream while others take notes. What makes God happy are those who listen to His word and turn it into action. It won't do any good if God's words are bouncing around in your head and they never see the light of day.

Be a doer. Don't be a pew sitter. God needs your hands and feet to do His work.

December 20

Knoweth

Therefore to him that knoweth to do good, and doeth it not, to him it is sin.

James 4:17

You know what is needed to further God's kingdom. If you stand by and refuse to help, then you are sinning. There's plenty to do, so pick something you can do.

I love to tell children Bible stories, so when Vacation Bible School comes around, I volunteer.

I love to cook, so when my Sunday school class did a fundraiser, we sold homemade soup, breads, and desserts. We raised enough money to build a church in Ghana, Africa.

I love sports, so I did a display for Ghana and got church members to bring old or new sports equipment. I also bought swing blades to help them cut their grass. These are only a few things that we will send, but it shows them how much we care and how much God cares for them. It means the world to them.

Show your love for others by helping show the love of God. It could save a life.

December 21

Charity

And above all things have fervent charity among yourselves: for charity shall cover the multitude of sins.

1 Peter 4:8

Here is another verse where God tells us to get involved in charity. If we don't have a heart for those in need, then we need to correct our heart. We are not to be self-centered. We need to teach our children to share, so that when they grow up, they will want to continue to share with others. It's harder to teach an adult to share.

Invest your time in children, they are our future. Don't forget those in need during the holidays. While buying groceries, you can buy an extra ham or turkey or cook a dessert for someone in need. You will be blessed as well.

December 22

Prosper

Beloved, I wish above all things that thou mayest prosper and be in health even as thy soul prospereth.

3 John 1:2

God wants us to prosper because He wants what's best for us. He's up there waiting to pour blessings all over you. Neither, does He want bad health for you. God wants to build you up, not tear you down.

If you get sick, you may have to alter what you've been eating. It's always best to eat fresh foods, instead of packaged products. In the Bible, they didn't have processed foods. Drink lots of water and you'll be feeling better soon. Also, keep your hands washed.

God loves you and wants you well, but you need to help Him.

December 23

Heaven

And God shall wipe away all tears from their eyes: and there shall be no more death, neither sorrow, nor crying, neither shall there be any more pain: for the former things are passed away.

Revelation 21:4

How are we going to feel when we get to heaven and realize that some family members and friends didn't make it? Maybe, we will realize that God is fair and just and that everyone had an opportunity. Maybe, we'll cry for a short period of time and then God will wipe away our tears.

I'm looking forward to no more pain, since I'm in constant pain here. We will no longer have a decaying body. We won't have a body that will ever experience death again. It will be a glorified body. Thank God for such a wonderful plan.

God is so much smarter than the rest of us. He is a divine being that has seen everything and then some. Thank God today for His plan and for His security. Have you told Him today, how much you love Him? Now is an excellent time!

December 24

Love

Love is of God.

1 John 4:7

I was sitting with my grandfather as he was dying and my grandmother walked in the room and started talking to him. The love they had between them was so sweet. I couldn't keep from crying as I listened. A few hours later, he passed away. Over 60 years of marriage had come to an end. Most marriages don't even last for half that.

The love you have with God doesn't last for a time frame, like a marriage, until death do us part. Our love with God, last for an eternity. An unconditional love that most of us never experience here on earth.

God loves us so much, He sent His only Son Jesus Christ to earth, so that the world might be saved. Jesus was your gift from God. What is your gift to God?

December 25

Merry Christmas

And she brought forth her first born Son, and wrapped Him in swaddling clothes, and laid Him in a manger, because there was no room for them in the inn.

Luke 2:7

What a way for a King to be born! A stable with animals and a lowly manger for a bed. Did it matter to Jesus where He was born? No. He was focused on His mission. His home was in heaven with His Father and He knew He would be returning soon.

We will be going home someday. Only God knows the date and the hour. Spend some time furthering the kingdom.

Whatever you've gone through here, it will prepare you for what you'll be doing in heaven.

Celebrate this day as your gift from God. Thank Him for His sacrifice for you. It cost Him dearly! Merry Christmas!

December 26

My Attitude

The longer that I live, the more I realize the impact that my **attitude** has on my life.

Attitude, to me, is more important than facts.
Attitude is more important than the past, than education, than money, than circumstances, than failures, or successes.
Attitude is more important than what other people think, say, or do.
Attitude is more important than appearance, giftedness, guts, or will.
Attitude will make or break a home, a family, a church, a community, an organization, a company, or a person.
The remarkable thing, is, that I have a choice every day. I can choose the **attitude** that I will embrace for the day.
I cannot change the past.
I cannot change the fact that some people will act in a certain way.
I cannot change, what is going to happen, regardless of what I do.
The only thing I can do is to use, positively, the one thing that I have and that is my **attitude**.
I am convinced that life is 10% of what happens to me and 90% of how I react to it.
And so it is with me, you, and us.
Both of us are in charge of our own **attitudes**, if we choose, to be in charge of them.
The choice is ours.

December 27

Goals

Let us hear the conclusion of the whole matter: Fear God, and keep His commandments: for this is the whole duty of man. For God shall bring every work into judgment, with every secret thing, whether it be good, or whether it be evil.

Ecclesiastes 12:13-14

The whole duty of man is to keep God's commandments. That's a tall order for anyone. This would be a good time to read over the commandments again. We make it hard. We are humans and we will make mistakes. Thank goodness God will forgive us. There is plenty we can do, if we'll just learn to discipline ourselves. Believe it or not, there are other religions that are much stricter than our commandments. We can follow God's laws. Set the commandments as a goal for you to achieve. With the help of the Holy Spirit, you can reach your goal. God will be so proud of you. No time like the present to get started.

December 28

Heaven

From that time Jesus began to preach, and to say, "Repent: for the kingdom of heaven is at hand."

Matthew 4:17

Jesus quoted this verse at the beginning of His ministry. I don't think people knew what He was saying. Early on in the ministry, people thought He was crazy and even sent for His mother at one point. Jesus told His mother that this was what He was created for. She knew He was from God and there was a plan. I'm not sure Mary understood what that plan was, but she knew He was created for greatness.

What makes me so sad, is how people treated Him. There was no need to hurt Him like they did. Why beat a man that is going to be crucified? Nailing one to the cross should have been enough pain for anyone. I'm glad we don't have to live by the laws they had in His day. Talk about strict! Add that to your thankful list.

December 29

Principles

The moral principles and precepts contained in the scriptures ought to form the basis of all our civil constitutions and laws. All the miseries and evils which men suffer from vice, crime, ambition, injustice, oppression, slavery and war, proceed from their despising or neglecting the precepts contained in the bible.

Noah Webster

If all men lived by the laws in the Bible, we would have a whole lot less crime in this world. Evil hearts of men won't realize the almighty God and His awesome power till they have to bow down before Him at the Great White Throne of Judgment. They will have only themselves to blame for their demise. No words or deeds can save them at this point. What's so sad, is there will be some good people in hell. That's breaks my heart. If only they would listen to those witnessing to them now, before it's too late.

The Bible is all we need in the way of instruction. God covered it all. He knew what we would need to get us through this life. Read your Bible. Don't try to make a go of it on your own. You need God to survive.

December 30

Our Nation

We ask almighty God to watch over our nation...and may He always guide our country.

George W. Bush

    The United States needs all the help it can get when it comes to homeland security. This statement made by President George W. Bush was made on September 14, 2001, only days after the 911 attack. I watched that day unfold and I was in shock from the extent of the damage from New York City to Pennsylvania, to the Pentagon. How in the world did they pull off such a wide spread attack? We dropped the ball in several areas. We are dealing with a radical group that will stop at nothing to wipe us off the map. We need God more than ever.

    Many people prayed that day, some maybe for the very first time or in a long time. We need to pray without ceasing like Paul instructed us. Has God taken His hand of protection off our nation? I pray not! If we as a nation would stop letting groups take prayers out of our schools and dictate to us what we can sing or pledge in the schools, then maybe God will honor our prayers more. We need God every minute of the day and night. We have tolerated way too much evil to enter into our nation. Our country was founded on Christianity and we need to take a stand to protect it.

December 31

The Bible

Within the covers of the bible are all the answers for all the problems men face. The bible can touch hearts, order minds, and refresh souls.
Ronald Reagan

If any one ever doubted the faith of the founding fathers then they need to go back and read some quotes like this one from Ronald Reagan. Our founding fathers left England so they could come to America to worship as they pleased. They risked their lives coming over here and then suffered from the harsh winters. Many of them died. Would you have made the voyage with them? Is our freedom to worship as we please that important to you? It is to me. I thank God on a regular basis for my freedom. People died to get that freedom for me.

I call them heroes.

Ronald Reagan was a great leader and a follower of God. He was a wise man. I pray we will always have a Christian leader. As time grows worse, we're going to need strong Christian leaders. If we don't vote wisely in the future elections, we will suffer for it. Pray with me for godly leaders, we deserve it.

About The Author

Vera Simpson Gaines was reared in Houston, MS on a diary farm and now resides in Senatobia, MS with her husband Gary Gaines of 38 years. She graduated from Houston High School in 1967 and attended Miss. State Un. where she graduated in Jan. 1972. Mrs. Gaines taught elementary school for 7 years and worked in educational research for 8 years before being forced off the road due to health problems. Gaines started writing in 2002. Her first book *Call Me Jobulene* is about her trials and tribulations and how the Lord lead her through them. Her second book *Are You A Job In Modern Times?* was written to help victims of Katrina to rebuild their spiritual lives. Her third book *All Is Well With My Soul Daily Devotions* was written to help people with adversities to face each day with the help of God. Mrs. Gaines is actively involved in the Emmaus Movement and charities for Africa. Mrs. Gaines has two daughters, Dr. Heather Gaines Hardison from Collierville, TN and Tiffany Gaines Lambert from Olive Branch, MS.

Healing Promises

By Jesus' stripes I am healed. (1Peter 2:24)

It is God's will that I prosper and be in health, just as my soul prospers. (3John 2)

The Lord is my healer: (Exodus 15:26)

Jesus came that I may enjoy life and have it in overflowing abundance. (John 10:10)

As I serve the Lord, sickness is taken from my midst. (Exodus 23:25)

Healing is one of God's benefits. (Psalms 103:3)

Jesus is the serpent of the pole lifted up in the New Covenant for my healing and deliverance. (John 3:14)

God sent His word and healed me. (Psalms 107:20)

I pay attention to God's word, for it is life to my body and health to my flesh. (Proverbs 4:20-22)

God gives me good and perfect gifts. He has no sickness or disease to give me. (James 1:17)

As I submit to God and resist the devil, he must flee from me. Sickness and disease must flee from me. (James 4:7)

Jesus is able and willing to heal me. (Matthew 8:1-2)

Jesus can heal me through my believing, receiving, and speaking His word or through the touch of another believer who is empowered by the Holy Ghost. (Mark 16:18)

Jesus paid for all sin and sickness at Calvary. (Matthew 8:17)

Jesus is the same yesterday, today, and forever. (Hebrews 13:8)

Because the Lord is my refuge and habitation, no evil nor plague shall come nigh my dwelling. (Psalms 91:9-11)

I am redeemed with the blood of Jesus Christ. (1 Peter 1:19)

I am justified by faith, not the works of the law. (Galatians 3:13)

Jesus redeemed me from the curse of the law. (Galatians 3:13)

The blessings of Abraham have come upon me. (Deuteronomy 28:1-14)

Jesus legally redeemed me from the bondage of sickness and disease and every other work of the enemy. (Luke 13:10-17)

Jesus bore my grieves (sickness) and carried my sorrows (pain). (Isaiah 53:4)

Jesus was wounded, bruised, and beaten for my sins, sickness, and diseases. (Isaiah 53:5)

I discern the Lord's body and receive all that he has provided for me, including healing for my physical body.
(1 Corinthians 11:23-30)

To touch Jesus is to be made whole. I touch Jesus today through prayer and faith. (Mark 5:25-34)

The resurrection power of Jesus Christ flows from my tongue as I speak words of life. (Proverbs 18:21)

I have been given authority in the name of Jesus to speak to the mountains that I face. As I command the mountains of sickness, despair, hopelessness, and lack to be removed in Jesus' name, they must go and be replaced with the fullness of God's blessings. (Mark 11:22,23)

Because I meditate on the Word of God day and night, God's prosperity and success are overtaking me in all realms of life.
(Joshua 1:8)

The measure of faith God gave me is growing by leaps and bounds. (Romans 12:3)

Because my faith is growing, nothing is impossible unto me. (Matthew 17:20)

Jesus is moved with compassion on my behalf. He wants me healed because of His great love for me. (Matthew 14:14)

Satan cannot dominate or oppress my life, because Jesus came to set me free. (1 John 3:8)(Acts 10:38)

Just as God's grace was sufficient to cause Paul to overcome all of Satan's buffetings. Christ Jesus causes me to triumph in every area of life. (2 Corinthians 12:9,10)

I will rise above anything and everything the devil throws at me. Nothing can keep me down, for I am more than a conqueror in Christ Jesus. (Romans 8:35-39)

Today I will rise to new life from the depression and prostration in which circumstances have kept me. (Isaiah 60:1)

Jesus is the author of abundant life, while it is Satan who steals, kills, and destroys. (John 10:10)

The days of my life are seventy years and if by reason of strength eighty. (Psalms 90:10)

Long life is mine because I obey and honor my parents in the Lord. (Ephesians 6:1-3)(Exodus 20:12)

My obedience to the Lord prolongs my life. (Proverbs 10:27)

Scriptures Used

Acts:	16:9 (NRSV)
	17:27
	20:35
1 Chronicles:	16:11
	16:25
2 Chronicles:	15:2
	20:6
	20:17
Colossians:	1:11
	1:29
	2:6-7
	2:9 (TLB)
	3:2 (NLT)
	3:12-13
	3:15
	4:2 (TEV)
1 Corinthians:	1:25
	1:18
	13:47
	14:33
	15:50

2 Corinthians: 4:6
4:7
4:18
5:7 (NASB)
5:17
7:10
9:8
11:25
12:9

Daniel: 12:3

Deuteronomy: 4:31
13:3
30:19
33:12
33:27

Ecclesiastes: 3:1
4:9-10
12:13-14

Ephesians: 1:3
2:8
2:10
3:20-21
4:32
5:25
6:4

Exodus: 15:2

Ezekiel:	11:19-20
	18:31
	20:12 (NRSV)
	34:16
Galatians:	5:1
	6:2
Genesis:	2:15 (NRSV)
	9:13
	16:8 (NIV)
	27:2
	28:15
Haggi:	1:7
Hebrews:	3:4
	4:15
	4:16
	10:22
	11:1
	11:6
	11:11-12
	12:1
	12:2
	12:28-29
	13:1
	13:2
	13:5
	13:6
	13:8
	13:21

Isaiah:	26:3
	30:18
	38:17
	41:10
	42:6-7
	42:16
	43:1
	43:2
	43:10
	48:18
	54:17
	55:11
	58:9
	60:19
	64:8
	65:24
James:	1:3-4
	1:12
	1:17
	1:22
	3:2 (NRSV)
	4:8
	4:10
	4:17
	5:16
Jeremiah:	7:23
	29:11
	32:27
	33:3
Job:	23:12
	35:9
	41:22

John:
1:1
1:14
1:17
3:16
3:17
4:7
8:12
8:32
10:10
11:40
12:46
14:3
14:6
14:18 (NIV)
14:27
15:13 (NRSV)
16:33
20:28-29

1 John:
1:9
3:16
3:18
4:4
4:12
4:16

3 John: 1:2

Joshua:
15:12 (NIV)
23:11
24:15

Lamentations: 3:22-23

Luke:	2:7
	5:32
	6:31
	6:37
	9:23
	10:41-42 (NIV)
	11:13
	11:28
	12:5
	12:32
	15:10
	17:21
Mark:	4:39
	6:31 (NRSV)
	6:41 (NRSV)
	10:27
	12:32
Matthew:	4:10
	4:17
	4:19
	5:8
	5:12
	5:16
	5:44
	6:6
	6:21
	6:24
	6:33
	7:7
	7:13-14
	7:21
	8:8
	9:37-38
	10:30
	10:32-33

Matthew(cont.)
        11:28
        11:29 (NKJV)
        12:34 (NIV)
        16:27
        17:20
        18:20
        19:26
        19:30
        21:24
        22:39
        24:35
        24:42
        25:40
        28:20

Micah: 7:7

Nahum: 1:7

Numbers: 23:19

1 Peter: 1:6-7
            1:22
            1:24-25
            3:15
            4:8
            5:7

Philippians: 1:6
            1:21
            3:12
            3:14
            3:20
            4:11
            4:13
            4:19

Proverbs:	3:5-6
	3:13
	11:25 (NRSV)
	15:28
	17:22
	22:6
	23:23
	27:19
	28:27
Psalms:	4:7-8
	9:9
	16:11
	18:28
	22:19
	23:2-3
	23:4
	23:6
	27:1
	27:11
	28:7
	29:11
	31:21
	31:24
	32:8
	34:7
	34:18
	36:7
	37:7
	37:24
	37:34
	40:10
	46:1
	46:10
	51:10
	55:16
	55:22

Psalms(cont.)
    56:9
    56:11
    57:9
    59:9
    61:2
    62:1
    62:2
    77:11
    82:3-4
    86:11
    90:12
    91:14-16
    94:12-14
    102:1-2
    103:4
    103:12
    107:9
    118:24
    119:11
    119:12,16 (TEV)
    119:105
    121:1
    121:2
    142:1
    145:14
    145:18-19
    150:6

Revelation: 3:20
    4:11
    21:4
    22:20-21

Romans: 1:8
                   3:10
                   3:23-24
                   5:1
                   5:8
                   6:4
                   6:23
                   8:6
                   8:15-16
                   8:26
                   8:28
                   8:31
                   8:38-39
                   10:9
                   10:17
                   12:2
                   13:8
                   15:13

1 Samuel: 16:7
                   25:6

2 Samuel: 7:18

1 Thessalonians: 5:11
                   5:18

2 Thessalonians: 2:13
                   5:16,17

1 Timothy: 4:8

2 Timothy: 2:2
             2:7
             3:1
             3:14
             4:5
             6:10

Zechariah: 2:10
             9:12

Zephaniah: 3:17

CPSIA information can be obtained
at www.ICGtesting.com
Printed in the USA
JSHW031544241220
10523JS00001B/1

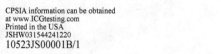